Equine
Law
&
HORSE
SENSE

Equine Law & HORSE SENSE

Julie I. Fershtman
ATTORNEY AT LAW

HORSES & THE LAW PUBLISHING
Franklin, Michigan

Book & Cover design: Patrick J. Powers, Ann Arbor, Michigan

Library of Congress Catalog Card Number: 95-81890
ISBN: 0-9648430-0-5

Direct written inquiries to:
Horses & The Law Publishing
P.O. Box 250696
Franklin, Michigan 48025-0696

Direct telephone inquiries to:
Julie I. Fershtman, Attorney at Law

810 644-8645 – telephone
810 644-8344 – fax
Fershtman@aol.com – E-mail

*To my husband Robert
for his patience and
understanding.*

Warning and Disclaimer

PLEASE READ CAREFULLY

In producing this book neither the author, publisher, nor distributor are engaged in rendering legal services. People receive legal servies and legal advice during a mutually-established attorney-client relationship where a client has given an attorney specific facts.

This book is also not intended to encourage you to become a "do-it-yourself" lawyer. However, it may help you better work with an attorney to achieve your goals.

Please keep in mind that the general legal principles discussed in this book may differ in each state, and exceptions may exist. The continuing challenge of the practice of law is that laws constantly change and new cases continue to be decided.

Contents

About the Author

Julie I. Fershtman is one of the best known equine law practitioners in the United States. Her law practice, based in Bingham Farms, Michigan, serves individual horse owners, insurance companies, trainers, instructors, associations, sales companies and agents, stables, breeders, and businesses across the country. Her expertise also includes insurance law, business and employment disputes, and real estate.

Ms. Fershtman's equine law practice has been featured in the national press, including *The Detroit Free Press, The Chicago Tribune, Texas Bar Journal, Lawyers Weekly USA,* and others. In 1995 the American Bar Association's *Barrister Magazine* named her one of "21 Young Lawyers Leading Us Into The 21st Century."

Active in community and bar association activities, she is the 1995-96 Chairperson of the State Bar of Michigan's oldest and largest section. She has organized law-related service projects that received awards from the American Bar Association.

Ms. Fershtman's biography is listed in *Who's Who in American Law* and *Best's Directory of Recommended Insurance Attorneys.* She is a 1986 graduate of Emory Law School and a 1983 graduate of Emory College.

Ms. Fershtman is a frequent lecturer at major national conventions including the American Horse Council, Equine Affaire/ Great American Horse Exposition, North American Horsemen's Association, North American Riding for the Handicapped Association, Equitana USA, American Riding Instructor Association, North American Horse Spectacular, and the National Conference on Equine Law.

Ms. Fershtman is widely known for her equine law articles, which have appeared in over 40 publications across the country. She also has written articles for *Equus* and *Horse Illustrated.* A horse enthusiast for many years, she has earned several awards and championships in horse show competition.

Preface

This book is written by a horseperson, first, and a lawyer, second. When I began my career as a lawyer in 1986, my goal was to eventually combine my life-long passion for horses with my training and education as a lawyer. However, law school never taught "equine law" and there were very few current books on the subject.

Not only was I left disadvantaged by the shortage of equine law information, but so was the horse industry. As a lawyer, however, I can research the law. The public is not so lucky; without accessible, understandable information, many people are forced to learn law the hard way — often after costly legal battles. With this in mind, in 1991 I began sharing information with the horse industry through a series of articles discussing a variety of legal issues. I also began lecturing at conventions across the country.

Equine Law & Horse Sense is designed to fill a need within the horse industry for a book that presents general legal principles in a down-to-earth and understandable way. The book combines a discussion of law with every day "horse sense" to help people avoid disputes. With the information this book provides, people may be more able to know when to seek help and how to work better with their own lawyer.

To everyone who has supported my equine law practice, my articles, or contributed in some way to this book, I sincerely thank you. It is my hope that this book will better inform you about law and help you continue to use good "horse sense" for many years to come.

Julie I. Fershtman, Attorney at Law
Bingham Farms, Michigan
November 1995

PART ONE

INTRODUCTION

What is Horse Sense?

What is "horse sense"? It is basic, practical common sense. It is the ability to apply sensible and reasoned approaches to certain problems that we encounter in our daily lives. Horse sense does not come with years of education or an advanced degree. All it takes is the willingness to think carefully and act prudently.

Horse sense belongs with horse activities. Sometimes having a general understanding of the law can help people use better horse sense and avoid problems that create legal disputes. Horse sense can prevent problems from becoming worse. This book may assist you when you need a handy source of general legal information and some "horse sense" on a variety of horse-related topics.

Every horse facility runs the risk of becoming the target of a land use challenge. Part 2 of this book explores some of these challenges and how basic horse sense can help avoid them.

Land Use Disputes

A land use challenge can originate from the local government, such as the City Council, which typically has authority to enact zoning and land use laws. These laws (known as "ordinances") can impact a horse facility several different ways. For example, ordinances can control the number of horses allowed per acre of land, dictate minimum acreage or lot sizes where horses can be stabled, change population density categories within an area, or modify setback requirements (the distance in which fences or structures must be

3

"set back" from a property boundary). Local governments can freely change land use ordinances, including ones that affect horses. Unfavorable ordinances or changes can ruin the future of horses within a community.

People *can* avoid undesirable zoning changes within their communities. Actively working with and for the community and striving for mutually-respectful relations with neighbors are horse sense efforts that pay off in many ways. Part 2 offers a few simple and practical ideas. In fact, this author follows her own suggestions in the community where she and her horses have resided — a highly-developed suburb located near Detroit, Michigan.

Even if the local government raises no issue with your horses, a land use challenge could originate from your own neighbors. All horse facilities are threatened with the possibility that a neighbor might one day bring a "nuisance" lawsuit. Lawsuits of this type attack the operations of a home, farm, or stable as being highly offensive, due to odors, sights, and sounds. If successful, a nuisance lawsuit can close or curtail the challenged operations for good. Part 2 demystifies the nuisance lawsuit and offers some suggestions for avoiding it.

Presently, nuisance lawsuits are not common in the horse industry. As we fast approach the 21st century, however, the threat of a nuisance lawsuit is more serious than ever. Urban sprawl is turning peaceful country settings into populated subdivisions and developments. People who move near horses, despite their desire to live in a rural-like environment, may not enjoy or understand them. For these reasons, the horse industry needs to become familiarized now with the law of nuisance.

Part 2 also discusses the problem of trespassers. The sheer disruption and annoyance they cause may be enough for anyone to abandon horse sense in dealing with them. Laws in many states allow both civil and criminal legal proceedings against a trespasser. A criminal proceeding is brought by the prosecutor who seeks to convict the wrongdoer and punish him or her with fines, jail sentences, or both. By comparison, the aggrieved person directly brings a civil proceeding, which seeks money from the wrongdoer as compensation.

Equine Business Mistakes

Part 3 addresses two major issues that have troubled equine businesses for years. By nature, an equine business is incredibly demanding and often consumes nearly every waking moment. Any trainer, boarding stable, breeder, or riding instructor will tell you that there are never enough hours in the day; even worse, weekends — a time when many businesses slow down or close operations —are usually the busiest times for the equine business. For these reasons, major business decisions are almost always handled at the last minute and sometimes in a hasty manner. Amidst the chaos, it becomes easy to forget that in the eyes of the law equine businesses are no different from any other business.

Equine businesses demonstrate good horse sense by knowing when to seek professional guidance. Having a general understanding of certain laws can help the process. All it takes is one hasty and poorly informed business decision to generate a lengthy legal dispute that will disrupt business, impair customer relations, destroy friendships, and cost huge sums of money in legal fees.

The first issue addressed in Part 3 is the innocent (but frequently wrong) assumption made by many equine professionals and businesses that their workers are "independent contractors" and not employees. To the busy equine professional, the independent contractor designation saves paperwork and money that would otherwise be spent on worker's compensation insurance, witholdings, benefits, and taxes, all of which are normally associated with keeping employees.

Unfortunately, businesses never learn until it is too late that the independent contractor is not merely a label but a special and mutually-understood working relationship. When a court or the Internal Revenue Service discovers an improper independent contractor designation — usually after a lawsuit or a tax audit — the legal and financial consequences can be very harsh.

The second issue explored in Part 3 involves debt collection. Virtually all equine boarding facilities will, at some point, encounter a customer who fails to pay his or her boarding fees. Stables are usually unaware of century-old state laws, often termed agister's lien or stablemen's lien laws, that were enacted to regulate this very situation. Ignoring the applicable lien law and improperly selling off a boarder's horse (even if only to recoup a few hundred dollars) can be a very costly mistake that might require spending thousands of dollars in legal fees to correct. These disputes have the potential to become a complicated five-way battle involving the stable, boarder, horse buyer, breed registry, and (sometimes) the police.

Equine Sales Disputes

Do you know people who have become permanently soured on horses simply because they had a terrible experience buying their first horse? Unscrupulous horse sellers have been with us for centuries, beginning with the days when horses were the sole means of transportation. They remain with us today, and their prime targets are first-time horse buyers who know very little about horses, and are eager buy right away. Part 4 begins with a practical guide to buying your first horse. The suggestions might even help people who already own horses make better informed purchase decisions.

Contracts & Releases

Tradition has been important in the horse industry. However, some traditions must change with the times. In the 1990's — the age of the "information superhighway" and when practically everyone has more affordable access to a personal computer than ever before — common horse-re-

6

lated transactions too often retain the character of the 1890's handshake deal. Although people know that well-written contracts can save money, avoid misunderstandings and financial liability, and prevent legal disputes, people still hesitate to use them when buying, selling, boarding, training, leasing, or breeding horses.

Part 4 explores common elements of several equine contracts. This book does not include form contracts, and there are four main reasons for this:

First, where equine matters are involved, "one size" simply cannot fit all — certainly not in the 1990's. For example, 35 states have passed laws in recent years that, in some form, control or limit certain liabilities for equine activities. About 21 of these laws require equine professionals and others to include special languagewithin their contracts and releases. Standardized form contracts will almost certainly miss this required language.

Second, every person or facility has unique interests and needs and, consequently, deserves a unique contract. "One-size-fits-all" contracts run a serious risk of failing to address these important and individualized needs.

Third, "one-size-fits-all" contracts can be unfair to either or both parties. In a sales transaction, as a prime example, the buyer and seller typically have opposing interests. Form contracts favor a middle ground which intentionally abandons many of these interests.

Finally, the author of a form contract is clearly not *your* lawyer and has no idea what your legal needs are. Your lawyer can advise you of your state's legal requirements and the best ingredients for your contracts.

Part 5 is devoted to releases of liability (sometimes called "waivers"). We have all heard someone say: "releases are not worth the paper they're written on." This is, in most states, a myth. Actually, most states *have* enforced liability releases that were properly drafted and presented. Only a small number of states have laws or judicial pronouncements that do not enforce releases.

Despite the incredible power and cost savings that releases offer, these documents remain seriously misunderstood throughout the horse industry. People who could benefit from releases avoid them. Worse yet, many people who use releases find themselves in the same position as those who never have. This happens when someone uses a recycled, outdated, improperly signed, or poorly-written release form that ultimately proves powerless in a legal challenge.

Good horse sense can help you resolve the confusion and misunderstanding frequently associated with liability releases. It begins by seeking the right information to separate fact from fiction. In this connection, you will need to make sure that your release complies with the unique requirements (if any) of your state's law. You should also find out who can legally sign a release and how a release should be presented. Part 5 will help get you started; your own attorney can do the rest. Keep in mind that having a release will not relieve you from the need to buy proper liability insurance.

Avoiding Liability

Part 6 of this book is devoted to equine-related liabilities. Good horse sense involves confronting and understanding the concept of liability and what causes it. Part 6 examines how the law generally allows people to sue for personal injuries in horse activities. It discusses the "cutting edge" trends and developments of the various state equine liability laws as well as negligence, the "attractive nuisance," and premises liability.

Understanding what may create liability is an important first step. Beyond this, horse owners, professionals, and facilities should plan ahead and take active measures to *avoid* the conditions that could generate a lawsuit. Part 6 includes several suggestions for avoiding liability and handling an incident that may arise.

Proper insurance is not only good horse sense, it is good business sense. Mortality, major medical, or loss of use insurance can save your finances in the unfortunate event that your horse becomes injured, ill, or dies. In our litigious society, liability insurance has become a must for everyone — from the individual horse owner to the highly sophisticated equine business.

Part 7 is devoted to equine insurance. It discusses the types of insurance that are popular in the horse industry. This section will help you work better with your agent to select the right types of insurance. Part 7 will help you maximize the full value of your insurance by explaining five pitfalls that sometimes cause people to lose their insurance coverage and encounter disputes with insurance companies.

Dispute Resolution

In the 1990's, the old saying: "I'll see you in court" is becoming less common. Nowadays, alternatives to the traditional court system (lawyers often term them Alternative Dispute Resolution) have become more popular than ever. Part 8 discusses the three most common alternatives — arbitration, mediation, and small claims court. Arbitration and mediation, in particular, have grown rapidly in popularity mainly due to the tremendous speed and cost savings they offer. Each alternative has its distinct benefits and disadvantages, many of which are addressed in Part 8.

In keeping with the emphasis on inexpensive and fast ways to resolve disputes, Part 8 discusses how to draft a demand letter. A demand letter is often used as a prelude to a court case in an attempt to alert another party to the existence of a dispute and to demand that it be resolved. Sometimes, a carefully written demand letter can resolve a dispute quickly and spare both parties the trouble and expense of proceeding further.

Laws & Legal Terms

Equine Law & Horse Sense was designed to keep complex legal terminology to a minimum. Because legal terms are sprinkled throughout the book, the glossary in Part 9 defines them. The glossary covers over 80 different legal words and phrases, including commonly misunderstood terms not discussed in this book such as "class action."

Good horse sense involves keeping aware of important laws that directly affect your equine activities. Equine activity liability laws are sweeping the country and, as of November 1995, are in 35 states. The laws differ in various ways. Part 10 lists and cites them.

Using Horse Sense

The never-ending desire for self-improvement —whether by reading this book, joining organizations, or seeking advice from knowledgeable people and professionals — is indeed a true reflection of horse sense. Although this book was designed to generally introduce you to some of the legal issues affecting the horse industry, it was not designed to provide individualized legal advice. Keep in mind that legal advice is given in a mutually-established attorney-client relationship in which a lawyer understands the facts of your particular legal matter.

PART TWO

THE LAW & EQUINE FACILITIES — FROM BACK YARD TO COMMERCIAL

PROTECT YOUR RIGHT TO KEEP HORSES IN YOUR COMMUNITY

Many years ago horse facilities were plentiful and nestled in peaceful country settings. In recent years, however, "urban sprawl" has permanently changed this scenario. What were once riding stables and bridle paths have become subdivisions and shopping centers. More than ever before, horse facilities now find themselves very close to large, new developments, and the neighbors may not appreciate horses.

If you sense that your community is becoming more resistant to horses and might be exploring possible zoning changes, are there efforts you can make now to maintain things as they are? Yes. Your strategy might not be a costly, lengthy legal battle but rather a way of life designed to avoid one. Instead of an open checkbook, you will need energy and positive action.

Your Own Horse Protection Strategy

I personally undertake my own "strategy" every day in my own community of Franklin, Michigan, which is a small, rural-like village situated 15 minutes north of Detroit. Affectionately called "the town that time forgot," Franklin is bordered by busy cities and major highways. However, totally unique to its suburban location, Franklin has a respectable number of two and three acre lots that stable horses of many breeds. The neighborhood grocer will hold your horse at the sidewalk while you shop for lunch.

In 1991, the Franklin government considered changing Franklin's horse ordinance to make it more difficult to stable horses in the community. As a concerned horse owner, I led a group of horse supporters who successfully blocked the measure.

Let me share with you some easy, practical suggestions on how you might address the issue of zoning changes in your own community:

1. Get Active in Your Community

Actively participate in community groups that sponsor worthwhile events. Every community has several. The goal is to meet others and show them that you're a reasonable, likeable person who shares their concerns for keeping the community beautiful and maximizing property values.

Remember that community organizations often serve as "feeder" groups for community government. Those who work with you could, sooner or later, end up on your City Council, Planning Commission, or Zoning Board of Appeals. They'll remember you. You might become one of them. To my surprise, I became one of them in 1993 when the Franklin Village Council appointed me to serve on the Planning Commission. As a Commissioner for two years, I helped the Franklin government evaluate new land use ordinances. Some of the proposed ordinances directly affected horse owners such as the large animal ordinance and ordinances relating to fence types and locations.

2. Keep Your Horse Facility as Neat and Clean as Possible

Who would argue that a neat, properly-maintained horse facility threatens property values or the safety and health of the community? Opponents of "horse-favorable" zoning eagerly seek visible examples of why horses detract from property values. Don't even give them a chance. Start with your own facility. The opportunities are endless: remove horse droppings from the road, paint the barn, clean out all rubbish, relocate manure piles away from view, plant grass seed, add flowers, touch up the fencing.

3. Keep Your Non-Horse Neighbors Happy

Who typically leads the battle against horses in suburban communities? Disgruntled neighbors who have never owned a horse. The day may never come when they share your love of horses, but you cannot afford to ignore them. Make all of your neighbors comfortable with your horse facility. Consider sharing with them your plans to install fencing or structures near property borders, even if you have no legal obligation to do so. Be reasonable with them. Try to understand their concerns.

In my experience, after negotiation with a neighbor I relocated part of my new pasture fencing. The loss of pasture space was a very worthwhile long-term investment. My neighbors are happy, they have enjoyed my horses, and they respect — and have never forgotten —the fact that I accommodated them.

4. Be Responsible

If you live in a community like mine where horse facilities are not common, remember that you're in the public eye every minute. Respect others' property and privacy. For example, don't trample or cut across someone else's property without permission. Set an example for other horse owners in your area.

5. Get Organized

Without a doubt, in any battle involving horses and zoning there is strength in numbers. In Franklin, horse owners like me know that the struggle to keep horses in the community could repeat itself in the future. Therefore, the slightest hint of trouble should find you actively seeking out your allies, whether they are horse owners or horse admirers. Why wait? Drive (or ride) around the community to find properties that stable horses. Introduce yourself. Exchange phone numbers. Share information about local government candidates known to have "anti-horse" or "pro-horse" leanings.

Conclusion

All of these suggestions are designed to start you on your way to protecting and defending the presence of horses in your community. As a practicing attorney, I firmly believe that common sense ideas, when properly implemented, can prevent legal battles from occurring. Use them well.

THE "NUISANCE" THAT COULD PERMANENTLY CLOSE A HORSE FACILITY

It is a well-known fact that a single 1,000 pound horse will produce about 10 tons of manure each year. Can a nearby landowner bring a lawsuit seeking to close a horse facility or curtail its operations simply due to the smell of manure or some other reason? Yes. In bringing such a lawsuit, that neighbor must prove that the facility was kept or maintained in such a manner as to create a *nuisance* that improperly interfered with the use and enjoyment of his or her property.

Nuisance lawsuits occur rather infrequently. However, "urban sprawl" over the years has turned riding trails into residential real estate developments. Many people, it seems, have moved to the country seeking a more rural-like way of life; yet, these people do not like horses. This creates the setting where nuisance lawsuits could potentially crop up.

What is a "Nuisance"?

"Nuisance" is broadly defined as any activity that arises from an unreasonable, unwarranted or unlawful use by a person of his own property which produces a material annoyance, inconvenience, or discomfort to another nearby landowner or to the public.

Over the years, people have brought nuisance lawsuits to attack horse facilities for circumstances ranging from offensive odors and intolerable noises to unsightliness or filth. The parties who bring these types of lawsuits can be one nearby landowner (who may bring a "private nuisance" claim) and/or a group of persons such as residents of a subdivision (who may together assert a "public nuisance" claim).

Regardless of the circumstances challenged by the complaining person [known as the "plaintiff"], a nuisance lawsuit will not succeed in most states unless the plaintiff can prove that the nuisance:

(1) arose from a condition in which the nearby property was used in a wrongful or unreasonable manner (or, as one court put it, "a nuisance may be merely a right thing in the wrong place, like a pig in the parlor instead of the barnyard");

(2) caused *substantial* harm to the plaintiff or his property; or

(3) *materially interfered* with the plaintiff's use and enjoyment of his property.

Successfully defending a nuisance lawsuit can be difficult for horse facilities, and some of the most obvious defenses may not always work. For example, the defense that the plaintiff willingly exposed himself to the nuisance conditions or "came into the nuisance" by moving to the area has been proving unsuccessful over the years.

The National Right-to-Farm Laws

Forty-two states now have right-to-farm laws, which are designed to protect specific types of agricultural operations from certain nuisance lawsuits. The right-to-farm laws vary across the country but tend to fall into two distinct categories:

Some of the laws provide that the agricultural operation will not be deemed a nuisance when the surrounding area has "changed conditions" or if the operation was established first and operated at least one full year before the surrounding area changed.

In other states, such as Michigan, the right-to-farm law creates a rebuttable presumption (or legally recognized inference which can be overcome with certain evidence) that the agricultural operation is not a nuisance as long as its has complied with certain accepted farming practices and environmental regulations.

18

Resolving a Nuisance

If the plaintiff can successfully prove that a horse facility is a nuisance, the next issue will be how to remove or "abate" it. In very rare and extreme cases, courts have abated the nuisance by terminating a horse facility's operations altogether. Eighty years ago, a court shut down the operations of a breeding farm after residents of a nearby residential area complained that the stable, particularly as horses were bred, generated offensive noises and sights. That court also took into account that the complained-of breeding activities occurred in plain view of children who resided in the area.

The more frequent remedy courts apply is to somehow accommodate the interests of all parties involved. A court may, for example, order a horse facility to actively eliminate the odors, alter its facilities, or reduce the number of horses on the property. Only in a very small number of cases nationwide have horse facilities been ordered to pay money to the plaintiff who has won a nuisance case.

Conclusion

If you suspect that your facility may become the target of a nuisance lawsuit, or if you believe you have the grounds in which to bring one, please keep the following ideas in mind:

1. A general feeling of dislike or discomfort resulting from the use of nearby land may not be enough to bring a successful nuisance lawsuit. Rather, courts will generally look for a land use by the defendant that "*unreasonably interferes*" with the interests of the plaintiff's use and enjoyment of land. Also, courts tend to examine nuisance cases from the sensitivities and sensibilities of a "reasonable person."

2. Since, depending on the severity of the alleged nuisance, courts will inevitably try to resolve the matter through a compromise, the parties should consider attempting to resolve the matter between themselves. The middle ground the parties reach on their own might be more practical than one ordered by a judge who does not understand horses.

3. The facility's best protection from nuisance claims or from a municipality's attempt to create new zoning ordinances unfavorable to horse owners might simply be good stable management and basic common sense. For several practical suggestions, read "Protect Your Right to Keep Horses in Your Community," which is found in Part 2 of this book.

4. Every nuisance dispute is unique. Parties on both sides of these disputes should seek the advice of a knowledgeable attorney.

FIGHTING BACK (IN COURT)
AGAINST THE TRESPASSER

Can a landowner or occupier of land bring a lawsuit against trespassers seeking money from them because of their unlawful entry upon the land? In many states, yes. Someone who trespasses on your property may not only be answerable to the police and criminal authorities for breaking the law, he or she might also be answerable to you for damages, payable in money, resulting from the unlawful trespass.

What is a Trespass?

A "trespass" is generally defined as any intentional use or invasion of another's real property without authorization and without a privilege recognized by law to do so. Some examples of a trespass are: a business customer refuses to leave your property after you have requested him or her to do so; someone wrongly remains in possession of your property after the end of a lease or other arrangement; a public officer has exceeded his or her authority to enter the premises; a family has turned your bridle path into a camping ground.

When a trespass occurs, most states allow the landowner, or person in legal possession of the land, to bring a lawsuit against the intruder. This type of lawsuit is not a criminal proceeding in which the object is to put the intruder in jail or impose a criminal fine. Rather, the lawsuit is a *civil* proceeding in which the object is to compel the trespasser to pay money (also called "damages") because of the trespass. A lawsuit of this type might also seek an order from the court to keep the trespasser away from the property in the future.

21

What Damages Can Be Recovered?

Courts tend to measure damages on a case-by-case basis depending on how the trespasser invaded the property and the financial loss, if any, the trespass may have caused. Also, courts in some states may allow the landowner to recover the value of his or her discomfort and annoyance caused by the trespass. If a court is inclined to award this type of compensation, the amount of money that a court may find appropriate will vary with the circumstances.

In many states, the law allows a trespass lawsuit to proceed *even* if there has been no actual damage to the property. Those states presume that the landowner suffered at least nominal damage from the unlawful interference.

Defenses

If you are the one accused of trespassing, your defenses could include that you had a legally valid right to enter the property, or a very important reason necessitated your entry on the property.

The fact that you did not know you were trespassing or the fact that you acted in good faith may not be as powerful as you think in defending a trespass lawsuit. Many states will hold you legally responsible for the mere act of trespassing on someone else's property, even if you did not realize you were trespassing and even if you did not foresee the damage you caused.

Conclusion

In conclusion, please keep these concepts in mind:

1. Persons with legal title or possession of property can sue others for trespass. This means, for example, that a landlord and a tenant can *both* bring a lawsuit. The tenant could sue for interference with his or her right of possession; the landlord could sue for damage to the land.

2. Many states have laws that address how to remove certain types of trespassers (such as former tenants who have overstayed their welcome). Also, statutes may exist relating to certain types of trespasses that damage certain types of land such as timber, mineral rights, orchards, or others. Therefore, consult with a knowledgeable attorney and check your state laws carefully before beginning a trespass lawsuit.

3. The law generally allows you to use only "reasonable force" to remove a trespasser from your property. Excessive physical force is usually only justified if the trespasser is threatening immediate serious harm.

4. If a trespasser refuses to leave your property after being asked to do so, the safest approach is to quickly summon the police to intervene.

PART THREE

SPECIAL EQUINE BUSINESS ISSUES

INDEPENDENT CONTRACTOR OR EMPLOYEE:
IT PAYS TO KNOW THE DIFFERENCE

Succeeding in the horse industry nowadays is tough. Expenses are high. Competition is fierce. Labor costs are high. Making a profit, it seems, is harder than ever. Wouldn't it be attractive to eliminate the high costs that come with keeping employees? Many equine facilities believe that they can cut these costs by simply labelling their workers "independent contractors" instead of "employees." Does this sound easy and legal? *Careful,* it may be neither.

There are major differences between employees and independent contractors, and the tax and legal consequences of making an improper designation can be very serious. Equine facilities usually learn this the hard way after they receive a challenge from the Internal Revenue Service (IRS), government agency, or a person hurt on the property, all of whom may assert that the worker was really an employee.

The Advantages of Independent Contractors

Independent contractors are *not* employees. By definition, an independent contractor is one who carries on an independent business and contracts to do some work for another according to his or her own methods, and without being subject to the control of the other as to the means by which the result is accomplished, but only as to the result itself. Consequently, one who hires an independent contractor is not responsible for paying the charges normally associated with employees, such as FICA, withholding, overtime, worker's compensation, insurance, and benefits.

27

Another advantage of independent contractors is that the employer will generally not be liable for the negligent or wrongful acts committed by the independent contractor or the independent contractor's employees. A classic example of the independent contractor is the handyman who brings his own tool box, does the work independently on his own or with his own workers, and leaves after the job is done or when it is too late to continue working.

When is an Independent Contractor an Employee?

The courts and the IRS have weighed a variety of factors to determine whether an independent contractor really is an employee. Some of these factors are discussed below:

• *Control.* This is probably the most important test. The courts and the IRS will examine the degree to which the facility controls the worker's work processes and work schedule. That is, the more the employer has supervision, direction, and control over the worker, the greater the chance that the worker will be deemed an employee. Also, the worker who receives training, instruction, assistance, and materials from the employer is more likely to be classified as an employee.

• *Continuing Relationship.* Workers who devote a large portion of their time, over an extended period, to one employer will more likely be regarded as employees. Independent contractors, by comparison, typically make their services available to the general public on a regular basis and are generally free to work when and for whom they choose.

• *Payment.* A worker paid by the hour, week or month tends to be regarded as an employee. On the other hand, payment by the job or by commission (or if a lump sum payment is made in installments) can reflect an independent contractor.

• *Assistants.* If the worker pays for his or her own assistants to perform part of the work, this could evidence an independent contractor relationship.

• *Other Factors.* Several years ago, the IRS issued Revenue Ruling 87-41, which was designed to guide employers in the factors the IRS may use to determine whether a worker qualifies as an employee or an independent contractor. This document, and others issued since, are useful resources to help the serious equine business person take appropriate action.

Conclusion

In conclusion, please keep these concepts in mind:

1. Just because you have labelled a worker an "independent contractor" does not necessarily mean that the IRS or the courts will agree. The factors described above can give you some idea of how you may fare in an IRS or legal challenge.

2. The independent contractor has several important obligations, such as self-employment tax, estimated tax payments, worker's compensation, and individual health and pension benefits. Terminated independent contractors cannot collect unemployment compensation.

3. If you have decided that a worker is an "independent contractor," make sure it is mutual. For example, find out if the worker has bought insurance and is handling the obligations described above.

4. Consider having an independent contractor understanding drawn up in a contract. There is never a guarantee that the courts will accept your designation, but the contract at least evidences your understanding.

5. An improper classification, by IRS standards, is a costly one. Even well-intentioned mistakes can receive harsh IRS penalties. A willful failure to comply with the law can expose employers to severe financial penalties.

6. Employment relationships raise several unique issues. Direct your questions to an attorney or Certified Public Accountant.

THE PROBLEM OF COLLECTING UNPAID BOARDING FEES

Let's examine the scenario of unpaid board from opposite perspectives:

On one side, you own a stable that boards and trains horses. One of your customers is now two months behind in payments. You want your money or else you want the customer's horse out of the barn. There seems to be a solution — someone wants to buy the horse, and she has offered to pay you the full amount of the debt in exchange for the horse and its registration papers.

On the other side, you own the horse and admittedly owe the stable board for two months. However, you just lost your job and your finances have suddenly become strapped. You believe you will have the board money in a week or two and could make future payments as they become due.

Horse owners and stables are often surprised to learn that laws in most states address this very situation.

What is an "Agister's Lien"?

Stables of all types and sizes should be aware of the agister's lien statutes in their state. An agister's lien, which is sometimes referred to as a "stablemen's lien," is a security interest in a horse that arises by operation of law when the horse's owner or another person acting on the owner's behalf leaves the horse with a person or stable for its care and keeping. For this reason, states typically do not require an express agreement to create the lien.

30

Agister's liens are similar to mechanic's liens. However, unlike mechanic's lien laws, most agister's lien laws were enacted during the 19th Century when horses were the sole means of transportation. Consequently, many of the agister's lien laws are outdated.

Forty-eight states, as of November 1995, have laws on the books designed to address agister's or stablemen's liens and how to enforce them. These states are Alabama, Alaska, Arizona, Arkansas, California, Colorado, Connecticut, Delaware, Florida, Georgia, Hawaii, Idaho, Illinois, Indiana, Iowa, Kansas, Kentucky, Maine, Maryland, Massachusetts, Michigan, Minnesota, Mississippi, Missouri, Montana, Nebraska, Nevada, New Hampshire, New Jersey, New Mexico, New York, North Carolina, North Dakota, Ohio, Oklahoma, Oregon, Pennsylvania, South Carolina, South Dakota, Tennessee, Texas, Utah, Vermont, Virginia, Washington, West Virginia, Wisconsin, and Wyoming.

Michigan's agister's lien statute, codified at Michigan Compiled Laws § 570.185, *et seq.*, states that whenever any person delivers a horse (or mules, cattle, sheep, and swine) to be kept or cared for, the caretaker (referred to in this article as the "lienor") has a lien for the value of charges incurred in the keeping and care of the animal.

How and When is the Lien Enforced?

Agister's lien laws do not allow stables to simply sell off a boarded horse and pocket the proceeds at their whim. Rather, the laws allows stables to enforce the lien after a *specified period of time* has passed and after the stable has followed certain *specific procedures*, such as letters, affidavits, notices, special sales, and sometimes court proceedings.

Michigan's statute, for example, provides that the horse's owner must have consented or agreed to allow the lienor to keep and care for the animal. Therefore, if a trainer or other person places a horse in the care of the lienor without the owner's consent, this might invalidate the lien.

Lien statutes across the country differ in the amount of time that must pass before the stable can legally sell off the boarded animal to satisfy a debt. Michigan's law requires that the animal must remain in the lienor's possession without payment for *nine months* before the lien can be enforced through sale of the horse [M.C.L. §570.187]. Laws in many other states provide for substantially shorter time frames.

The state statutes provide different methods in which the stable must notify the animal owner that the animal is about to be sold off to pay the debt. Michigan requires that *thirty days* before the sale the lienor or someone on behalf of the lienor must send a registered letter to the owner of the horse, or the person who delivered the horse to the stable, at his or her last-known address. Michigan's law provides exact language for the letter, such as who is claiming the lien; the horse over which the lien has been asserted; the amount that the stable asserts is now overdue for care of the horse; the amount that will be due in thirty days when the horse is scheduled to be sold; the fact that the lienor has scheduled a public sale in thirty days; and the date, time, and place that the public sale will take place.

Must the Stable Keep Possession of the Horse?

An agister's lien is almost always a possessory lien, and the stable usually must retain possession of the horse in order to enforce the lien and collect money from a sale.

What should a stable do if the laws of its state do not require keeping possession of the horse to enforce a lien? Stables situated in these states must decide whether to part with a horse or keep it until all boarding charges are fully paid. This decision becomes even more important if the stable intends to seek remedies (such as a sale) under a lien law. Under these circumstances, stables should look to their state law. Michigan's agister's lien statute provides that the stable/lienor "*may* retain possession of the [horse] until such charges are paid" [M.C.L. § 570.185].

Before agreeing to allow the owner to remove a horse when boarding fees have not been fully paid, a stable will need to evaluate a few concerns. One concern is the likelihood that the stable can collect money from the boarder in the future. If it seems apparent that selling off the horse will be the only way to satisfy a debt, the stable would be wise to keep possession of the horse. Another concern is whether the horse's likely sales price will cover most or all of the unpaid boarding fees. If the debt far exceeds the horse's value, and the stable cannot legally sell the horse right away, it might be wise to part with the horse rather than allow the uncollectible debt to increase.

Stables that are permitted or required by law to keep possession of a horse before selling it off must contend with certain legal duties. The most important duty is to give *reasonable care* to the boarded horses belonging to all customers, including customers who have not paid their boarding fees.

What Type of Sale Must Take Place?

The state's lien law may dictate the type of sale that the stable must hold. Michigan's law allows the stable to sell the horse to the highest bidder through a "public sale" if the owner, or other person on the owner's behalf, does not pay the overdue boarding fees by the sale date. The "public sale" requirement in Michigan is satisfied by having a constable or court officer conduct the sale in a public place [M.C.L. § 570.187]. A private sale to a friend, as in the scenario above, would likely violate the Michigan law but might be completely lawful under another state's law.

An important element of the lien laws is that they almost uniformly address how the owner should be notified that the stable intends to sell off his or her horse. This is not coincidence; this is compliance with basic constitutional legal principles. State laws can specify how, or if, the stable must advertise the sale and/or notify the horse's owner before the sale occurs. In this connection, many of the laws go into great detail and mandate the exact wording of the notice letter, the time frame between notice to the owner and the sale, the manner of sending the notice letter, and the types of public advertisements required.

Buyer Beware

Buying a horse through a stablemen's lien sale can be a risky venture. Several problems could occur: the former owner might refuse to transfer the horse's registration papers to the buyer's name, and the breed registry could refuse to accept a transfer of ownership without the former owner's written approval. Even worse, if the sale has been conducted improperly, the former owner might accuse the buyer and/or the stable of theft and demand immediate return of the horse along with money as compensation for the inconvenience. Some former owners have sought criminal charges against the seller and the new owner!

Many breed registries have policies permitting the transfer of ownership of a registered horse without a signed transfer form. However, for their own protection, these registries will demand reliable and compelling proof (such as a Court Order or an attorney's opinion letter) that the sale fully complied with the applicable state's agister's lien law.

Before bidding on a horse that someone purports to sell while acting under an agister's lien statute, demand to know what procedures the lienor has followed before the sale, who has the papers, and the name and address of the last owner.

What if The Sale Brings Too Much or Too Little?

Unfortunately, agister's lien sales rarely generate enough money to pay off the boarder's debt to the stable and the costs of holding the sale. However, state laws address the circumstance in which the stable might derive extra money from the sale.

Michigan's agister's lien statute prevents the lienor from earning more than the amount of the debt plus costs and expenses of the sale [M.C.L. § 570.187]. Michigan law also requires the stable to deposit extra money with the clerk of the city or township where the sale took place, and then notify the (former) owner so that he or she can claim the money [M.C.L. § 570.187].

Before deciding to sell a horse, the boarding facility should evaluate whether the state law permits other collection measures to be taken in the event that the sale fails to bring sufficient funds to cover the debt. Michigan's law, for example, allows the lienor, even after the sale, to collect any balance due by suing the owner [M.C.L. § 570.188].

Alternatives to the Agister's Lien

• *Collection Lawsuit*

Instead of an agister's lien sale, the stable/lienor usually can sue the horse's owner or responsible person to collect the debt.

Sometimes the mandatory waiting periods are simply too long to make the stablemen's lien remedy desirable. For example, Michigan's nine-month waiting period, which is required before a stable can sell a horse, makes a collection lawsuit the more reasonable option for many facilities. A collection lawsuit can be brought quicker than the nine-month waiting period before the sale. On the negative side, however, the stable might be forced to sue again to recover new charges that accrue after the first suit ends.

If a stable brings a successful collection lawsuit against a boarder, the court will issue a judgment that orders the owner to pay a certain sum of money to the stable, plus interest. Then, the boarder can either pay the judgment or take an appeal to a higher court within a certain time, usually about a month from the date the judgment was issued. After that time passes without appeal, the judgment becomes legally enforceable, and the stable can pursue several actions allowed by law to collect money. These actions could include garnishing the boarder's wages or seizing and selling off certain assets belonging to the boarder; the horse might qualify as such an asset. The stable should be sure to check the state's laws and procedures to make sure that any seizures and sales are appropriately carried out.

• *Language in a Boarding Contract*

Stables are well-served by having boarders sign carefully

written boarding contracts *from the beginning.* The contract might include procedures the stable must follow if the boarder falls behind in board payments. Where allowed by law, a boarding contract might include reasonable remedies and provisions that are more favorable and more specific than those found in the state's lien statute.

Stables might also, where allowed by law, want the boarding contract to specify charges that the stable can recoup if it sells off a horse to satisfy a lien. Those charges might include attorney fees, consignment fees, hauling expenses, and others.

For the horse owner's benefit, a boarding contract might, for example: specify a favorable grace period for board payments; prevent the sale of the horse until a lengthier number of weeks or months has passed; allow the stable to sell the horse only after the stable has made several different attempts over time to reach the owner, such as contacting the owner by phone *and* sending a letter to the owner at one or two different addresses.

For obvious reasons, the stable and boarder have different interests on the subject so they will surely disagree on terms if they negotiate a contract.

Conclusion

In summary, please keep the following ideas in mind:

1. If you own or operate a stable, make sure that you strictly adhere to the procedures outlined in your agister's lien statute, unless you are permitted by law to enter into a contract allowing you to proceed differently.

2. The stable and boarder are always free to settle the unpaid board problem in a mutually-agreeable way. Going back to the scenario at the beginning of this article, a payment plan might solve the matter. The parties should consider consulting with legal counsel, especially if the settlement involves promissory notes, interest payments, consent judgments, secured transactions, new contracts, or modifications of old contracts.

3. Stables should keep and update records of all boarders' names, addresses and telephone numbers. When someone delivers a horse claiming to act on the owner's behalf, the stable should obtain the names, addresses, and telephone numbers of the owner and someone likely to know the owner's whereabouts.

4. Agister's lien laws vary considerably across the country. Check the law in the state where your stable is located.

Note: Several legal issues involving liens are not addressed above. These issues include possible conversion liability where the stable has sold the horse in violation of state lien laws or other laws, what happens if competing liens are asserted on the same horse, Article 9 of the Uniform Commercial Code (which covers the subject of secured interests), constitutional issues such as due process, and many other legal issues.

PART FOUR

EQUINE TRANSACTIONS AND CONTRACTS

A PRACTICAL GUIDE TO BUYING
YOUR FIRST HORSE

Caveat emptor or buyer beware. We know these caution-
ary words. When it comes to buying horses, people too easily
forget them. The horse industry, just like any other industry,
has its "bad eggs" who will take advantage of inexperienced
buyers. Unscrupulous horse sellers have existed for centuries,
when horses were the sole means of transportation, and they
remain with us today, when horses are a hobby.

First-time horse buyers are usually not prepared or
equipped to handle the smooth and clever tactics of an unscrupulous horse seller. First-time buyers tend to have no
ties to the horse industry, are generally unfamiliar with the
value of a horse, cannot spot the warning signs of an unsound horse, and are usually eager to buy right away. As it
often turns out, first-time buyers cannot recognize — until
after they have parted with huge sums of money — the an-
tics of an unscrupulous horse seller.

Here are 10 suggestions designed to help people protect
themselves when buying their first horse:

1. Never Deal on a Handshake

What if the seller tells you a horse has "absolutely no bad
habits," is "100% sound," and has "never been sick or lame"? A
seller who makes these or other promises in regard to the horse's
current and past condition should have no hesitation putting it
in writing.

Written sales contracts protect buyers many different ways.
Consider hiring a lawyer to draft a sales contract for you or

41

to review the contract a seller may ask you to sign. Also, Part 4 of this book discusses "The 5 Minute Sales Contract."

2. Never Buy With Cash

Cash sales are trouble waiting to happen. The unscrupulous seller who insists on cash could later deny ever receiving it. Unless the cash deal is combined with a well-written contract that acknowledges the seller's receipt of the full sale price, stick with a check or money order.

3. Have an <u>Independent</u> Veterinarian Inspect the Horse Before the Sale

A veterinarian can perform a pre-purchase examination on a horse, which is designed to test the horse's overall health and condition. At your request, and for an extra fee, the veterinarian can perform specific tests during the pre-purchase examination. For example, the veterinarian can X-ray the horse's legs (usually the front feet, fetlocks, pasterns, and/or hocks) to detect certain types of degenerative lameness conditions such as Navicular Disease. Depending on the breed of the horse and your intended use, the examination can also involve ultrasound tests, neurological tests, and blood work.

Whenever possible, choose an independent veterinarian who is not familiar with the horse and does not work for the seller. Try to attend the pre-purchase examination. The veterinarian can share observations with you as he or she makes them. Keep in mind that some horses may act a bit nervous around a veterinarian (horses, like people, can be scared of the doctor), but this is a good opportunity to further observe the horse's behavior.

4. Blood Tests

Unscrupulous sellers have been accused of tranquilizing or medicating horses in order to mask behavioral or soundness problems. To check for this, the veterinarian can collect blood and/or urine samples during the pre-purchase examination. The veterinarian will forward the samples to a laboratory, which can detect substances.

5. Consider a Trial Period

Buyers can request a "trial period" which would allow the buyer a week or more to test out the horse before the sale concludes. However, even the most ethical and sincere seller may decline your request because trial periods can be risky for the buyer and the seller. This is especially true if the buyer plans to move the horse somewhere else during the trial period. For the protection of both parties, get a carefully-written agreement detailing the obligations of each party during the trial period. The contract can, at a minimum, reflect payment, insurance, the buyer's restrictions (if any) in using the horse during the trial period, and the quality of care the horse must receive.

6. Get To Know The Horse

With the cooperation of the seller, visit the horse more than once and watch it in several different settings:

- *First thing in the morning.* How does the horse act when he is "fresh"? If he is broke to ride, what type and amount of preparation does it take before he can safely be ridden?

- *Saddling (or harnessing) and bridling.* There may be a reason why the seller wants you to wait while this is done somewhere else.

- *In the stall.* Watch the horse in his stall for a while. Does he crib (suck wind)? Does he kick the stall walls and doors? Does he lunge out aggressively at people who walk by? How are his manners while being fed?

- *In the arena.* The "test ride" may reveal only part of a horse's performance abilities. When this occurs, chances are good that you and the horse will be alone in an arena or field. This is a nice start. However, if you plan to ride or show the horse near other horses, it might help to simulate those conditions.

43

- *Trailer Loading.* Some horses are poor loaders. This is a problem if you anticipate doing a great deal of hauling to trail riding events, competitions, shows, or other activities. Sometimes a difficult loader can be corrected, but it will take time and money, especially if you need to hire a professional trainer. If hauling is important, ask to see the horse loaded in a trailer similar to the type you plan to use.

7. Get Advice

Consider asking someone whose opinion you trust to evaluate the horse. It always helps to receive advice from a well-respected person who is knowledgeable of horses and your intended use for the horse you hope to buy.

8. Read the Horse's Registration Papers

The horse's papers usually do more than reveal its age and lineage. Beyond this, the papers might show how long the seller has owned the horse (and whether the seller actually owns the horse) and the names of all people who have owned the horse since birth.

9. The Horse's Performance Record

Do you plan to show the horse? Most first time horse buyers prefer a seasoned show horse. If you know the horse's breed and registration number, most breed associations or registries will send you the horse's performance history. This information will tell you what awards the horse received in competitions recognized by the breed or organization and when they were received. These records will not include results from certain unrecognized events such as local or open shows.

10. Ask Questions

By following the suggestions above you will have plenty of questions to ask the seller.

Conclusion

The phrase *caveat emptor* (buyer beware) is not meant

to suggest that buyers have no legal rights. They do. Aggrieved buyers can sue sellers for breach of contract, fraud, and other things. Also, most states now have laws that prohibit unfair and deceptive trade practices in consumer transactions. These laws can be very powerful; many of them allow the buyer who wins a case to recover treble (triple) damages and, in some cases, attorney fees. If you suspect that you were wronged by a seller, contact a lawyer right away.

By giving yourself plenty of time, planning ahead, and using good horse sense while buying a horse, you will be very satisfied with the horse you bought and you will have avoided a legal dispute.

The Five Minute Sales Contract (For People Who Would Otherwise Deal on a Handshake)

Has this scenario happened to you or someone you know?

The offer sounded too good: A "proven broodmare" in "sound condition" for sale now at a bargain price. Within minutes you paid the seller cash and, with the mare's registration papers and a transfer of ownership form in hand, hauled her away. A mere handshake sealed the deal.

Transactions like this are very common in the horse industry, and legal battles sometimes follow them. In the example above, the mare might turn out to be barren or unsound; the seller could demand money (since there is no record of your cash payment); someone else might claim they own the mare and demand her return; the seller might refuse to refund your money if the mare turns out to have none of the qualities you had understood. These disputes might have been avoided if the parties had a sales contract.

Sometimes, for any number of reasons, buyers and sellers have avoided or refused to use contracts. A common complaint expressed against contracts is that it takes time to prepare them. However, lack of time does not have to be an excuse. Within five minutes you can draft a sales contract that includes the most basic and essential elements of a horse sale.

Why Use a Contract?

Contracts can avoid misunderstandings by explaining major elements of the transaction. Without a contract, a dispute involving a horse sale is guaranteed to become a battle of words in which the buyer and seller have totally different understandings of the transaction. Contracts can eliminate the disputes altogether or narrow them significantly.

The process of entering into a contract can often reveal the other party's sincerity. That is, the buyer who promises to make payments over time or the seller who vows that a horse is perfectly sound ought to put it in writing if you so request.

Your "Five Minute Sales Contract"

The elements below are the *minimum* for a 'Five Minute Sales Contract ":

1. Parties

Who are the parties to the transaction? Specify the seller and buyer's full names, addresses, and telephone numbers. Minors under the age of 18 will need a parent or legal guardian to sign.

2. Horse

This is the subject of the sale; describe it clearly and avoid confusion. For example: "Scotty Straw, 1987 American Quarter Horse gelding. AQHA Registration No. 123456. Dark chestnut with blaze and three socks."

3. Price

Mention the sales price and state whether the seller has received full payment. If the buyer will pay over time, list each installment, exact due dates, where to send payments, and type of payments (check, money order, etc.). Specify when the buyer can take possession of the horse a n d / o r the registration papers. What can either party do if payment is not timely or properly made? Make sure to get this in writing.

4. Warranties

This element is up to you; before you elect to avoid warranties in your contract, at least understand what they are.

Sometimes the seller has made promises regarding the horse's qualities, which may be important to the buyer. In the situation above, the statement "sound condition" could be deemed a warranty that the horse conforms to the promise. Other examples of warranties include: "he does not crib," or "she has never taken a lame step." These are generally known as express warranties.

The buyer may want to get the most important warranties in writing. This would require listing specific statements the seller had made that the buyer has relied on. Under no circumstances should *anyone* buy a horse from someone who refuses to warrant in writing that he or she owns the horse (or is acting under full authority of the true owner as the sales agent) and can sell it to you.

What if the broodmare in the example above was unsound at the time of the sale or was suffering from a disease? As a matter of law, if a warranty proves to be false, the buyer may have grounds in which to legally rescind the sale and/or seek money from the seller (including, but not limited to, money spent on the care and keeping of the mare before it is returned to the seller or the difference between the price paid and the mare's true value). Usually the law places a burden on the buyer to notify the seller of the problem very soon after the problem is discovered.

There is a difference between a dispute involving warranties (usually known as a "breach of warranty" dispute) and a dispute involving fraud. To win a warranty case, the buyer need not prove that the seller knew the statement, or warranty, was untrue when it was made. By comparison, in a typical fraud case, the buyer must prove: that the seller *knew* the mare was unsound or not a "proven producer" at the time he or she made these statements to the buyer; the seller made the statements to induce the buyer to buy the mare; the buyer relied on the statements in deciding to buy the mare; and the statements were actually false.

Generally, laws usually allow sellers to disclaim or waive

the existence of warranties in a sales agreement by including language that they have made no warranties and/or that the horse is being sold on an "as is" basis. Sellers must be sure that these types of disclaimers are obvious and not hidden within a sales contract.

Recent developments in the law within many states, including Michigan, indicate that using "as is" language in sales agreements will not always prevent a seller from being sued for sales fraud. For example, in non-horse settings, many sellers have been found liable where they have used "as is" clauses in sales contracts but failed to disclose known flaws or defects in the items being sold.

Clearly, both parties to a sales transaction benefit when the buyer is allowed an opportunity to independently evaluate the qualities and condition of the horse being sold. The seller should welcome the opportunity for the buyer to have a horse inspected by a veterinarian or equine professional before the sale is completed. To encourage this, the seller might want to include language in the contract to this effect.

5. Signatures

Both parties should sign the sales contract. If the other party claims to be signing on behalf of a business, make sure he or she has authority. Also, if one party is a minor, make sure that his or her parent or legal guardian signs.

Conclusion

These suggestions for a "Five Minute Sales Contract" are designed to help you document horse sales which would otherwise be made on a handshake. More complete sales contracts, which will protect you better, take longer and can be drafted by a knowledgeable attorney. If you have questions about sales contracts or any aspect of a sales transaction, direct them to an attorney.

Note: *Several laws and legal issues involving sales, such as Article 2 of the Uniform Commercial Code, are relevant to equine sales but, in the interests of simplifying the issues, have not been addressed above.*

Protection of Horse Owners and Horse Facilities by Written Agreements

Has the situation below happened to you or someone you know?

Finally, you found the horse you have been searching for. The horse fits all your needs, except for the fact that it is over your budget. The seller seemed more than accommodating and took your deposit. He promised to keep "your" horse for another month until you were able to pay him the balance and then haul it home. He promised to have a veterinarian check out the horse for you. Contented, you gave the seller a $200 cash deposit and drove home without even a receipt.

Transactions like this occur very frequently in the horse industry. They are trouble waiting to happen, especially if any number of possible problems should occur. For example, the horse could be sold to someone else; the buyer might be dissatisfied with the seller's chosen veterinarian or the exam results; the horse could become ill before the buyer takes possession; the seller might refuse to refund your deposit or deny ever receiving it since there is no record of a payment. These problems could have been avoided if the parties had entered into a written contract.

Why are Contracts Beneficial?

Carefully written contracts can help protect all horse owners, professionals, and horse facilities against lawsuits, misunderstandings, and financial liability. As an old saying goes, "paper does not tend to forget."

When a transaction, such as a horse sale, takes an unfortunate turn, parties without a contract will almost certainly have different recollections of the agreement. However, had the parties signed a carefully worded contract that included important elements of the transaction and addressed potential problems, their dispute would have been prevented or severely limited.

The process of preparing a written contract, whether the contract is drafted by lawyers or by the parties themselves, forces the parties to think about and determine their respective rights and obligations. Also, the other party's willingness to enter into a written contract can be a good indication of his or her fairness and candor. That is, the seller who insists that a horse has never been lame or the buyer who assures you that he will make payments over time should be willing to put these statements and promises in writing if you so request.

Drafting a good contract is only a part of the process; the contract should be properly signed. Contracts signed on behalf of a corporation, for example, should include the corporation name, signer's name, and his or her title. A farm name, such as "Morningstar Farm," should not be used as a party to the contract unless it is a true legal entity; the unincorporated facility might be referenced, for example, as "John Doe, d/b/a [doing business as] Morningstar Farm."

Contracts signed by a company's employee or agent (the one who acts on behalf of another) should include the name of the employer or principal (the one who has hired another to act on his or her behalf). Also, if you enter into a contract that was signed by an employee, agent, or company representative, the law may impose on you the duty to determine the scope of that person's authority to execute the contract. Parents or legal guardians should sign contracts on behalf of minors.

Below is a discussion of certain types of contracts used in some horse-related transactions and many of the elements commonly found in each of them.

Boarding Contracts

Boarding contracts can protect *both* the boarder and the stable. These types of contracts can include, for example:

- Description of the horse boarded;

- Horse's mortality insurance carrier and emergency phone number;

- Representations regarding the horse's health (such as negative Coggin's Test, current inoculations, recent de-worming, etc.);

- Charges and payment obligations (boarding fees, veterinary and farrier services, late fees, etc.);

- Stable's discretion (or lack of discretion) to handle medical emergencies if the owner cannot be reached;

- Release of liability, where allowed by law;

- Participation in any de-worming or inoculation programs arranged by the stable; and/or

- Usually if requested by the boarder, the standard of care the stable will attempt to give to the boarder's horse.

The parties to a boarding contract can also, at their discretion, insist on the right to terminate the boarding arrangement upon certain conditions, which the parties can make as limited or as specific as they want.

Equine Leases

Like leases involving real estate, leases involving horses can avoid many problems *before* they occur by addressing the problems and by specifying each party's obligations.

The parties to an equine lease are the "lessor" and the "lessee." The lessor owns the horse and has agreed to allow the lessee to use it subject to the terms of the agreement. An equine-related lease can include, for example, the following:

- Description of the horse involved;

- Amount and frequency of payments to the lessor;

- Permitted uses of the horse during the lease term (such as riding, driving, breeding, showing, or racing);

- Rights of either party, if any, to assign the contract to someone else;

- Maintenance of the horse during the lease (including, for example, who pays the boarding stable, trainer, farrier, or veterinarian);

- Who bears the risk of loss if something should happen to the horse during the lease term;

- Obligation, if any, to procure certain types of insurance on the horse, such as mortality or major medical and surgical insurance;

- Obligation, if any, of the lessee to procure certain types of liability insurance while the lease is in effect;

- The standard of care regarding the horse during the lease term;

- Releases of liability, where allowed by law;

- Indemnification provisions, where allowed by law, which are designed to protect the lessor from liability or financial loss arising from occurrences that arise when the lessee uses or has possession of the horse;

- Actions that can be taken (also called "remedies") if either party fails to honor certain important obligations in the contract; and/or

- How and when the parties will end the lease and how the term of the lease can be extended.

For a more detailed lease, other possible provisions can include:

- The lessee's option to buy the horse during or at the end of the lease;

54

- How certain care and veterinary issues will be addressed (such as who will pay for a major veterinary procedure that becomes necessary during the lease term);

- The lessee's right to sell the horse and how the proceeds will be distributed; and/or

- Specific restrictions, if any, on who can ride, train, board, or handle the horse or the activities for which the horse can be used while the lease is in effect.

Breeding Contracts

Over the years, stallion owners have used several different types of breeding contracts. For mare owners, the wide range of breeding contracts and the variations in their terms make it more important than ever to read each contract very carefully. The mare owner must determine exactly what the stallion owner is offering in exchange for the stud fee and what the stallion owner expects from the mare owner.

Stallion service contracts typically offer a one-time breeding right to a stallion (the breeding of which is sometimes called a "season"). The most common stallion service contracts are the "guaranteed live foal" or "in foal" contracts, although some stallion owners, especially in the racing industry, offer "no guarantee" breeding contracts. A "guarantee" breeding contract involves a refundable fee or a right to a re-breed if the mare fails to produce a "live foal." On a national level, the definition of "live foal" has taken on a variety of meanings and varies from breeder to breeder. Most "live foal guarantees" guarantee only a foal with the ability to stand and nurse; other contracts define "live foal" as the ability of the foal to stand and nurse after a certain specified period of time, ranging from 24 to 72 hours after birth.

An "in foal" contract is a variation on the "guarantee" contract, in which the stud fee is paid if the mare is conclusively determined to be in foal after a 42-day exam. After that, should the mare, for any reason, fail to produce a live foal, there is no refund or right to re-breed the mare free of charge.

A "no guarantee" stallion service contract typically involves a non-refundable stud fee, usually paid before the breeding, and no opportunity for a free re-breed to the stallion if the mare fails to produce a live foal.

Other types of breeding contracts include, for example, "foal sharing" agreements in which the mare owner and stallion owner (or the owner of a syndicate share or breeding right) agree to breed the mare to the stallion with the understanding that the parties to the contract will co-own the foal. A variation of this type of agreement exists when the mare owner agrees to pay the stallion owner a sum of money after the foal is sold, which will satisfy the breeding fees and charges.

"Mare lease" arrangements have also become popular. These contracts resemble equine lease agreements, discussed earlier, but address other issues such as: ownership of the resulting foal, option to re-breed the mare if she fails to produce a live foal, insurance, payments, maintenance responsibilities, and other provisions.

A stallion service contract can include, for example, the following:

- Identification of the parties and descriptions of the stallion and the mare;

- Payment obligations, including how much is due and when;

- Representations regarding the stallion and mare (such as health, ownership, condition, etc.);

- With live cover breeding contracts, conditions under which the stallion owner or handler can refuse to breed the mare;

- When, or if, the mare owner can receive a refund;

- Provisions if the mare and/or the stallion specified in the contract cannot be bred due to death, infertility, or another reason;

- Releases of liability, where allowed by law; and/or
- Rights of either party, if any, to assign the contract to someone else.

Purchase and Sale Contracts

Horses are too frequently sold on a handshake, to the detriment of the buyer and seller. Written agreements can eliminate confusion and establish responsibilities.

Not surprisingly, the buyer and seller have completely different interests in a sale transaction and, undoubtedly, the terms proposed in the purchase/sale agreement vary greatly depending on whether the buyer or seller has drafted it.

A sales contract can include, for example, the following elements:

- Specific identification of the buyers and sellers and their respective names and addresses;
- Description of the horse to be sold;
- Price and payment terms;
- Date of sale;
- Place where horse will be delivered and who will bear the risk of loss from the time the contract is signed to the time when the buyer receives the horse;
- Warranty that the seller has ownership, title, and ability to sell the horse to the buyer; and/or
- Agreement to execute necessary documents with the breed registry or registries that reflect the transfer of ownership created by the sale.

The buyer and seller may also want to include or, alternatively, exclude (or "disclaim") representations and warranties regarding the health and history of the horse.

As the situation warrants, the purchase agreement can be combined with promissory notes, UCC financing statements, installment payment arrangements, and other documents. The parties can also consider addressing the issue of who should pay the sales taxes.

Training Contracts

A training contract can include, for example, the following:

- Fee schedules and payment obligations;

- Training services to be rendered;

  Location of the horse during training;

- Disclaimer of promises or warranties regarding the horse's future performance (which trainers may prefer); and/or

- Authorization for the trainer to sell the horse or, for race horses, to enter the horse in a claiming race.

Also, as obvious as it seems that the training process will place certain stresses on a horse, trainers might insist on language in their contracts in which the owner acknowledges this fact and signs an appropriate liability release (where allowed by law).

Various General Contract Provisions

Some general provisions that can apply to several different types of contracts include:

- Special remedies if a party to the contract wrongly fails to abide by his or her obligations, such as payment of court costs and attorney fees to the other party;

- Which state's law governs the contract;

- Where allowed by law, the location of any lawsuits that may arise out of the contract or the transaction about which the contract was created (also known as "venue");

- An optional agreement to submit any dispute arising

under the contract to binding arbitration at the election of either or both parties; and/or

• An acknowledgment that the contract is the complete expression of the parties' agreement and can only be modified in writing.

Conclusion

Contracts are unique to the parties and circumstances involved. While form contracts sold in stores and in books often contain helpful language, they run the risk of being too general and depriving the parties of needed language that protects them. For these reasons, people seeking the best protection in the contracts they use should have the contracts drafted or reviewed by a knowledgeable attorney.

TURNING A GOOD BOARDING CONTRACT INTO A GREAT CONTRACT

Could the following scenario happen to you?

You just returned from your dream vacation — a two-week cruise. You immediately dropped off your bags at home and rushed straight for the boarding stable to see your horse. But instead of greeting you, she was nowhere to be found. Her stall was empty. The stable owner approached you with the terrible news: Your horse had a very severe bout of colic the day you left, and the veterinarian recommended surgery immediately. The stable could not reach you to obtain your permission. With no way of knowing whether you would consent to the costly surgery, the stable owner told the vet to put down your mare. Later, while you were still recovering from the loss of your mare, you received another shock: the insurance company that issued a mortality policy on your horse advised you that it would not pay your claim because the company believed that you did not honor the policy's terms requiring giving proper and timely notice of your horse's illness.

Whether you view this tragic scenario from the perspective of the equine facility or the boarder, it is clear that nobody was a winner. These problems might have been avoided if the parties had a well-written boarding contract.

Are All Boarding Contracts Alike?

All boarding contracts are *not* alike. Some merely list the fees that the customer must pay and the stable's daily services. Details, however, can make all the difference. In the scenario above, the customer might have returned to find her mare alive if the boarding contract had included a few simple details.

Uncommon Elements of Boarding Contracts

The following are five ideas to consider (at a minimum) for boarding contracts:

1.Handling Emergencies, Especially with an Unavailable Owner

Veterinary medical emergencies, ranging from cuts to colic, are a foreseeable part of horse ownership. In the situation above, the horse owner could have given the facility, before the vacation, a phone number or instructions for handling emergencies.

The boarding contract presents a good opportunity for the facility to address handling emergencies. For example, the facility might want to request a broad authorization to procure veterinary attention if an emergency arises when the owner is unavailable. On the other hand, the owner might want to limit the authorization or give the stable special instructions.

2. Insurance

Is it the horse boarding facility's business to know that you bought a policy of mortality insurance on your horse? Yes. Equine mortality insurance companies will give you an emergency telephone number which you (or possibly someone in possession of your horse) must call if your horse becomes injured or ill.

Equine insurance policies typically require that the company must be notified promptly so that it can evaluate each problem, preferably while the horse is still alive. The insurance company may want to do any number of things such as consult with the attending veterinarian, order an investigation or new course of treatment, consent to have a horse put down, and/or order an immediate post-mortem examination.

3. Your Equine Activity Liability Act Language

As of November 1995, 35 states across the country have laws that, in some fashion, control or limit certain liabilities in horse activities. Many of those laws require equine-related contracts to include specific "warning" or other language. If required by the appropriate state law, make sure that your contract includes this language.

4. Facility-wide Equine Health Programs

What good is keeping your horse carefully immunized against transmittable diseases if the rest of the horses at the stable have fallen drastically behind in their inoculations? Boarding facilities may want to establish an inoculation and de-worming schedule for all horses. The boarding contract presents a good opportunity to list the schedule or to disclose the program and have all boarders consent to it. These provisions promote the general well-being of all horses on the premises, and boarders might actually insist on them.

5. Release of Liability
(if Allowed By Law)

Have you ever heard the statement: "Releases are not worth the paper on which they're written"? Chances are good that you not only have heard it but you have repeated it, without even knowing whether the statement was true under the law in your state.

In fact, most states have enforced liability releases, as long as they were properly written and presented. Boarding facilities in those states would be wise to include appropriate release language in their contracts in an attempt to limit their liability. Keep in mind that a release is a very important document that should be drafted with the assistance of an attorney. Having a release does not eliminate the need for proper insurance.

Conclusion

For the protection of the facility as well as its customers, the boarding relationship deserves a well-written contract. Facilities and their customers have different needs and interests where the boarding contract is concerned. It is strongly suggested that you have your boarding contract drafted or reviewed by a knowledgeable attorney.

EVALUATING YOUR BREEDING CONTRACT — WILL IT PROTECT YOU FROM DISPUTES?

Anyone in the horse breeding business can tell you that a wide variety of disputes can *and do* occur between the stallion owner and the mare owner. Sometimes these disputes turn into lawsuits. Some issues that have, over the years, divided stallion owners and mare owners are:

When can the mare owner get a refund and how much? When can a substitute mare or stallion be used instead of the horses specified in the contract?

What medical procedures will the stallion owner be authorized to arrange for the mare (such as routine palpation)?

What does the contract really mean by "live foal guarantee"?

If the contract requires live breeding (also called "live cover"), what happens if the stallion is sold or moves a great distance away before the breeding takes place?

All of these are critical and foreseeable issues. Both stallion and mare owners often learn, usually after a problem arises, that the breeding contract does not even address them.

Elements of Breeding Contracts

Consider the following 12 ideas, at a minimum, for your breeding contract:

1. Proper Signing and Descriptions of the Parties

The best breeding contract will fail if it does not properly describe the parties it involves and if the contract is not properly signed. Specify the mare owner and stallion owner together with their addresses. Avoid using the farm name as a party to the contract unless it is a legal entity. Where corporations are involved, the contract should include the corporation name, principal place of business, signer's name, and title. Parents or legal guardians should sign on behalf of minors.

2. The Horses and Breeding

Which stallion and mare will be bred under the terms of the contract? List them carefully, along with their respective registered names, breeds, registration numbers, tattoos and/or freeze brand numbers. You might also want to describe each horse by color and markings and list the sire and dam of each horse.

All it takes is one diseased mare to endanger every horse at a breeding facility. With live cover breeding, the breeding contract offers a good opportunity to include safeguards that protect the horses from disease or epidemics brought by a visiting mare. The mare owner might be required to promise that the mare is "current" as to inoculations and worming and is sound for breeding purposes; consider specifying (with a set time frame) what this means. For example, many stallion owners require mare owners to present a health certificate and negative Coggin's Test that was taken by a licensed veterinarian within 30 days or 60 days of the mare's arrival at the breeding facility.

Do the parties understand the range of dates or months in which the breeding should take place? This is especially a problem when one or both of the horses have a rigorous race or show schedule. Get it in writing.

3. Payment Obligations

List the stud fee, booking fee (if any), additional charges, manner of payment, and date(s) when payment is due. Check your state's laws regarding interest. Many form breeding contracts include high interest rates which, though perfectly acceptable for lending institutions, can be unlawfully high for equine-related businesses. Also, some states assess certain taxes on the breeding of horses. In those states, the parties should specify in the contract which party must pay them.

Disputes sometimes arise when the breeding facility arranges special services, especially veterinary services, for the mare without the mare owner's advance permission. Mare owners who refuse to consent to certain routine procedures, such as palpation or the removal of hind horseshoes, might want to specify this in the contract. Stallion owners, on the other hand, tend to prefer contract language authorizing the breeding facility to arrange, at its discretion, routine or emergency professional services performed by the facility's veterinarian or farrier.

4. Release of Liability, if Allowed
Under Governing Law

Stallion owners have every reason and incentive to give the best possible care to every mare brought to their facilities. Where allowed by law, however, breeding contracts can include a release of liability (also called a "waiver") pertaining to the mare while in the stable's custody. Keep in mind that having a release does not eliminate the need for proper insurance.

5. Don't Forget Your Equine Activity
Liability Act Language

As of November 1995, 35 states across the country have passed laws that, in some form, control liability in horse activities. Importantly, many of these laws require contracts used by equine professionals (such as horse breeders) to include certain language. If you live or do business in one of those states, now is a good time to make sure that your breeding contract includes the proper language.

6. Foal Guarantees

The three words "Guaranteed Live Foal" mean a great deal in the breeding industry; these words can also generate widely different expectations among the mare and stallion owners. Why invite guessing? Define these terms. Over the years, "live foal guarantee" has meant several different things: a foal that can stand and nurse; a foal that survives for 24 hours (some contracts extend this to 72 hours) after birth; or, if twins are born, the survival of one twin foal.

Some contracts, which are uncommon in breeding transactions, provide a "no guarantee" arrangement or guarantee only that the mare will be "in foal." Those contracts should very clearly and unambiguously specify these limitations.

7. Foreseeing and Addressing Possible Events

Whether you are the stallion owner or the mare owner, the breeding contract allows you the opportunity to address several foreseeable events, such as: the mare fails to produce a "live foal"; the mare is barren or dies before breeding or foaling; the stallion dies before the service; the mare or stallion is sold or moved a great distance while the contract is in effect; the mare or stallion is believed to be unsafe for live cover breeding purposes.

For these and other types of situations, the breeding contract can specify whether, and when, the mare owner can receive a partial refund, full refund, or re-breed with the same or a substitute mare. Some breeding contracts provide that the contract will become void if the stallion moves a great distance away from its location when the contract was originally signed or if the stallion becomes infertile; in those instances, the mare owner might be entitled to a refund of the stud fee. Other contracts give the stallion owner discretion to select a substitute stallion under these circumstances.

8. Enforcement of Contract Obligations, Including Payment

Many states have stallion owner lien laws designed to

help the stallion owner secure payment for breeding services. These laws, for example, give the stallion owner a lien on the mare and foal resulting from the breeding and require the stallion owner to undertake certain specified procedures before selling off either or both of them to enforce the lien. In some states, the constitutionality of these laws has been questioned. Consult with an attorney regarding the lien rights and secured interest laws. Some breeding contracts specify that the breeder's certificate will be withheld from the mare owner if the mare owner has somehow violated the contract or until breeding fees are paid in full.

9. Who Will Pay the Legal Fees if a Dispute Arises?

In many states, it takes specific language in the contract that creates an entitlement to legal fees before a court will award them to either party in a legal dispute. Consider specifying in the breeding contract that the prevailing party shall collect attorney fees and court costs from the other. Alternatively, since this type of language "cuts both ways," some contracts state that *only* the stallion owner shall be entitled to recover attorney fees and court costs if he or she prevails.

10. Boarding and Mare Care Issues

If the mare will be boarded at the stallion owner's facility, the stallion owner should ask the mare owner to sign a separate boarding contract. Otherwise, the language typically found in a boarding contract can be included within the breeding contract.

11. Insurance Requirements

Proper insurance protects both parties in a breeding transaction. The stallion owner should keep available the name of the mare's mortality insurance company, as well as the policy number and the insurer's emergency phone number. All of this information might be important if it becomes necessary to notify the insurer of illness, disease, or injury to the mare.

Equine facilities that board quality horses frequently purchase "Care, Custody, and Control" insurance, which is separate from the stable's general commercial liability insurance. This type of insurance offers coverage in the unfortunate event that a horse should become injured or die while in the custody of the boarding facility.

12. Other Language

Numerous other provisions can be included in breeding contracts, if allowed by law. For example, the breeding contract can specify the state whose law will apply or the location where legal proceedings may be brought. Also, contracts more frequently provide that disputes can be resolved through alternative methods of dispute resolution, such as arbitration.

To avoid the problem of one party attempting to change a contract through a verbal arrangement, consider requiring that the contract can *only* be modified through a writing that has been signed by both parties. These requirements are reasonable in the age of lightning-fast communication through telefaxes and overnight mail.

Conclusion

The time, effort, and expense of a proper breeding contract can avoid the expense and business disruption caused by a legal dispute. Stallion and mare owners should use a good breeding contract and follow the policies and responsibilities they have set within it.

PART FIVE

LIABILITY WAIVERS
OR RELEASES

CAN YOUR FACILITY'S LIABILITY RELEASE EFFECTIVELY PROTECT YOU AGAINST A NEGLIGENCE LAWSUIT?

This scenario is all too familiar:

The stable manager hands a new boarder, renter, or riding student a standard form release. The release is signed on the spot, nobody bothering to even glance at its language. Even the stable manager is not familiar with the release, and where it came from is anybody's guess. It could be a copy of a friend's form, or maybe it was copied from a book somebody bought at the tack shop, or possibly some body else's farm used it several years ago. Yet, as he files the signed release away, the stable manager might believe that the stable is now protected against liability if the signer is later injured. Is he?

More proof exists that liability releases in the horse industry *are* worth the paper on which they are written, and much more. In Michigan, for example, two noteworthy and recent cases reveal that courts are enforcing liability releases and dismissing personal injury lawsuits by people who have signed them. Both cases directly involve equine activities.

As reassuring as these cases may seem, they do not guarantee success for every horse facility. However, these cases help illustrate some guidelines that horse owners and facilities may consider as they evaluate their own releases.

The 1991 Michigan Federal Court Case

In 1991, a Michigan federal court ruled that a guest who signed a riding resort's liability release could not later sue for negligence after she fell from a rented horse. Accordingly, the Court dismissed the lawsuit — in which the plaintiff had sought over $50,000 against the resort—without even a trial.

In the case at issue, the defendant was a Michigan resort ranch which rented horses to its guests. The plaintiff was a guest who wanted to rent a horse for trail riding. Following its usual procedure, the resort asked the plaintiff to sign three documents.

The first document the plaintiff signed was a Registration Card, which included broad and general language releasing the resort from liability for all personal injuries. The second document was the stable's liability release. Some of the language in the release included:

- "I understand that horseback riding will expose me to above normal risks."

- "I agree that I am responsible for my own safety."

- "I agree that [ranch], their employees and agents will not be liable if I suffer personal injury or death, except if caused by their gross negligence or willful and wanton misconduct."

- The top of the release stated in capital letters: "PLEASE READ THIS CAREFULLY."

- The bottom of the release stated in capital letters above the signature section: "I HAVE READ THIS AGREEMENT BEFORE SIGNING IT."

The last document the plaintiff signed was a sign-up sheet, which stated: "All riding is at your own risk." The following day the plaintiff went on a trail ride at the resort. During the ride her horse bucked and she fell off, suffering permanent injuries.

What follows is any stable's nightmare. The plaintiff sued the resort. Her lawsuit claimed that the resort was negligent for failing to take certain precautions that would have made her ride safer and prevented the incident.

The resort, in defense, claimed that the release prevented the lawsuit. There was no issue that the plaintiff signed the release. She freely admitted this. However, she asserted that the release should be invalid because, in her own mind, she had no intention of releasing the resort from liability. The plaintiff also tried to invalidate the release by stating that nobody had discussed the documents with her or asked her to read them before she signed them.

The sole issue before the court was whether the plaintiff legally released away her right to sue the stable. Surprisingly, this was an unusual case for the Michigan courts since most other lawsuits involved releases signed *after* the plaintiff was already injured. (A classic example of these types of releases would be settlement agreements typically given in exchange for a lump-sum payment.) Here, in sharp comparison, the document at issue released the resort from possible *future* liability, and the plaintiff signed the release the day before she went riding.

The court was guided by Michigan law, which provided that a release is presumed to be invalid if: (1) the person who signed it was dazed, suffering from shock, or under the influence of drugs; (2) the release was misrepresented; or (3) there was other fraudulent or improper conduct by the party who benefited from the release.

Keeping these legal principles in mind, the court found no evidence that the resort had tricked the plaintiff into signing the release. The release was not represented to be anything other than what it truly was. Accordingly, the court held that the release was binding and dismissed the lawsuit.

The 1995 Michigan State Court Case

A similar case came before the Michigan courts and, in June 1995, a state court in Michigan dismissed a lawsuit against a northern Michigan riding stable. In that case, this author successfully defended the riding stable.

The defendant riding stable presented the plaintiff with a liability release before she rented a horse for a one-hour guided trail ride. The release contained language in which the plaintiff agreed to release the stable from liability for its own negligence. Many provisions in the release resembled the one in the 1991 case.

Within an hour after signing the release, and 45 minutes into the ride, the plaintiff fell from the horse. She claimed that the saddle slipped, but one eyewitness believed that the plaintiff simply lost her balance and fell off while cantering. There was no evidence presented that the saddle was defective. In fact, shortly after the incident the same horse with the same equipment went on another trail ride. The stable denied any wrongdoing.

As a result of the fall, the plaintiff suffered severe physical injuries, which required many surgeries and rehabilitation. She claimed that she was unable to return to her former employment and could only work part time for a much lower hourly wage. Through her attorney, she sought over $100,000 in damages to compensate her for the alleged permanent disfigurement, lost wages, and emotional pain and suffering. The plaintiff's husband also was a party in the lawsuit and sought damages for "loss of consortium."

Just as in the 1991 federal court case, the defendant stable asked the court to dismiss the case. The request (called a "motion") had plenty of supporting evidence and law. The plaintiff read and signed the stable's release, and there was no evidence that the stable misrepresented it.

The plaintiff, in response to the stable's motion, claimed that she had no real intention of releasing the facility from liability. However, the court looked to the plain language of the release, found no evidence that the stable misrepresented it, and, accordingly, dismissed the case.

Conclusion

As these two cases demonstrate, not only must the release be carefully drafted, but the manner in which it is administered can be equally important.

FIFTEEN IDEAS
REGARDING EQUINE ACTIVITY LIABILITY RELEASES

Most states allow people to use written releases (also called "waivers") in an attempt to limit their liability. In our litigious society, it is more important than ever to consider using liability releases, where allowed by law.

Here are fifteen ideas regarding equine-related liability releases, all of which are provided for reference only and do *not* constitute legal advice.

1. Readability

The release should be written in clear and straightforward language. A release that is broken up into separate paragraphs, instead of one very large and very long paragraph, can be easier to read.

2. Title

Reinforce that the release is a contract. In this connection, consider entitling the document a "RELEASE OF LIABILITY" or "WAIVER OF LIABILITY," or a "____ [specify the activity such as boarding, training, riding instruction, etc.] AGREEMENT AND LIABILITY RELEASE." These titles may help reaffirm to the reader exactly what you are asking him or her to sign.

3. The Persons Being Released from Liability

Identify the parties carefully. Some form releases simply allow you to fill your name in the blank as the party who is being released from liability. Do you want the guest, visitor, or customer to release from liability only one person? Usually not. In fact, chances are good that you want several people released from liability. For this reason, where the document names the people being released, do not just name the horse owner, equine professional, or stable — consider listing or mentioning people *associated* with them.

Where allowed by law, consider adding other names to the release. Since it is usually not possible to list other people by name, it is sometimes lawful to describe them by terms such as "Jane Doe Stables and its employees, agents, owners, and managers."

For *corporations*, consider mentioning that the other party is not only releasing the corporation but also its directors, officers, and shareholders.

For *organizations*, consider also mentioning that the other party is not only releasing the entity but also, for example, its directors, officers, and affiliated persons, volunteers, sponsors, and groups.

4. Who is Signing the Release?

Get the signer's full name, address, and phone number. Is the guest, visitor, or customer signing the release on behalf of himself/herself, his or her minor (under 18) child, legal ward, heirs, representatives, and assigns? This is important. Say so.

Remember that releases signed by minors are not legally binding so be sure to have *only* a parent or legal guardian sign.

5. Risks Presented by the Equine Activity

Does the signer know that equine activities are hazarous by nature and could expose him or her to serious injury or even death? To illustrate the point, and further reaffirm the inherent risks, consider describing some of the risks and including examples of many dangerous things that horses are capable of doing without warning. Many state equine liability laws will list "inherent risks" for you, which you can repeat in your release. However, be sure to mention that you are only providing *some* examples of horse-related risks.

6. The Heart of the Release

Clearly, the most important language in a release is the part where signers, on their own behalf and on behalf of their children or legal wards, agree to waive any legal rights to bring a lawsuit. Lawyers call this the "exculpatory language." The manner in which this part of a release is drafted usually determines the release's success or failure.

Cases in some states have indicated that liability releases should mention that the guest or customer is releasing the person or facility from liability that results from "ordinary negligence." Most states follow the principle that one cannot legally release another from the consequences of gross negligence, intentional wrongdoing, or wanton and willful misconduct. Check your state's legal requirements and make sure your release is fashioned appropriately.

7. Draw the Reader's Attention to Important Language

Consider drawing the reader's attention to the most important language, especially if your release is going to be pretty long. CAPITAL and/or **bold** letters can help achieve this goal, and they can be used in the important paragraph in which the guest, visitor, or customer agrees to release the owner or stable from liability.

8. Consideration

What can evidence the parties' intention to be bound? This falls, in part, under a legal principle called "consideration." Your release might address this by, for example, mentioning that the release is binding when the stable permits the visitor or customer to enter the property or engage in certain activities (such as receive lessons, rent a horse, ride on the premises, etc.).

9. Governing Law

To avoid any possible confusion about what state's law controls the release, specify the state whose law applies.

10. Equine Liability Act Language

The equine liability laws in many states include a special "WARNING" notice and, in some instances, require this language to be repeated in equine activity contracts and releases. Check your state's law to be sure.

Indiana's equine liability law, for example, provides that a written contract for professional services or for the rental of an equine or equipment must contain in clearly-readable print the following language:

WARNING

Under Indiana law, an equine professional is not liable for an injury to, or the death of, a participant in equine activities resulting from the inherent risks of equine activities.

11. Special Business Concerns

Many equine professionals and stables have special provisions included within their liability releases. Some of them include:

- Representations of the rider's physical condition. When drafting this, be particularly sensitive to the Americans With Disabilities Act, which could make it unlawful to implement a "screening process" that singles out people with certain disabilities and automatically excludes them.

- The rider's prior riding experience.

- An authorization for the stable or professional to seek medical attention for the rider.

- Many equine facilities, professionals, an individual horse owners explain to their customers about the benefit of wearing protective equestrian headgear (particularly ASTM-standard and SEI-certified helmets) during equestrian activities and while near horses.

- Facilities nationwide sometimes have policies requiring customers to have medical insurance, and some even require visitors to specify in writing their insurance carrier and policy number. Other facilities require customers to affirm in writing that they either have appropriate medical insurance or have suffcient funds to pay the costs of their own medical care if an injury should

12. Signature

Above the signature is a good section to acknowledge that the signer has read and understood the release before signing it. Also, check to determine if your state requires written releases to be signed by witnesses.

13. Presenting the Release

A well-written release could be found invalid if it has been presented improperly. When presenting a release, consider the following:

- Assess the person signing the release. What if the person who will ride or be near horses is a child? The release should be signed by at least one parent or legal guardian (usually the signature of one of them can be sufficient). It also goes without saying that someone appearing drunk or under the influence of intoxicating drugs should *never* be asked to sign a release, much less be allowed near your horses.

- Try not to rush people into signing. If you leave the room after giving out a release, consider asking upon returning: "Have you read it? Do you understand it?"

- Do not conceal that the document is a release of liability.

14. Insurance

Having a release does not eliminate the need for proper insurance. Also, in the unfortunate event that you are sued by a person who has signed your release, an insurance company can provide a lawyer and pay for your legal defense. Unfortunately, even if courts in your state have enforced releases, there is never an absolute guarantee that all judges will accept and enforce your release.

15. Remember to Seek Legal Advice

Each horse owner, equine professional, or facility has different needs for its liability releases. Some states will not enforce them. Therefore, consult with a knowledgeable attorney to draft, review, or update your release. The expense could be well worth it.

Conclusion

A release is a *very* important legal document. Over the years, however, releases have been the target of much misunderstanding. Some people believe that it is unnecessary to use releases as long as they post a sign that says: "Ride At Your Own Risk." However, there are important differences between this type of sign and a well-written release of liability. Certainly, a sign may plainly reveal the facility's policy of limiting its liability. However, after an incident arises, the injured party is almost certain to deny ever having seen or read it. A written release of liability, by comparison, is an affirmation *in writing* that a guest or visitor has read, understood, and agreed to accept the "ride at your own risk" policy. Also, anyone who verbally promises not to sue should not hesitate to put this in writing.

PART SIX

EQUINE-RELATED LIABILITIES
AND AVOIDING THEM

THE NATIONAL EQUINE LIABILITY LAWS

In the 1990's, the laws regarding equine activity liabilities have undergone major changes. As of November 1995, 35 states have equine activity liability laws on the books. In several ways these laws have permanently changed the nature of equine-related liability.

Many of the equine liability laws share common characteristics, but all of them differ. The laws were designed to, in some way, limit or control certain liabilities where personal injuries arise from equine activities.

Which States Have Equine Liability Laws?

States with some type of equine-related liability law are: Alabama, Arizona, Arkansas, Colorado, Connecticut, Delaware, Florida, Georgia, Hawaii, Idaho, Illinois, Indiana, Kansas, Louisiana, Maine, Massachusetts, Michigan, Minnesota, Mississippi, Missouri, Montana, New Mexico, North Dakota, Oregon, Rhode Island, South Carolina, South Dakota, Tennessee, Texas, Utah, Virginia, Washington, West Virginia, Wisconsin, and Wyoming. This list includes the laws as of November 1995.

Who Benefits from the Equine Liability Laws?

The laws tend to benefit stables, equine professionals (such as trainers, riding instructors, and breeders), and persons and entities that provide or sponsor equine activities. Many of the laws also benefit individual horse owners if they provide horses, equipment, or certain services to others, even if no money is exchanged.

85

How Do the Laws Limit or Regulate Liability in the Horse Industry?

Most of the laws reaffirm that equine activities come with certain inherent risks. The laws prevent equine activity participants and their families from bringing suit and recovering money if an injury or death results from an inherent risk. Typically the laws tend to go to great lengths to define "inherent risks of equine activities." Colorado's law, for example, states:

[T]hose dangers or conditions which are an integral part of equine activities . . . , including but not limited to:

(I) The propensity of the animal to behave in ways that may result in injury, harm, or death to persons on or around them;

(II) The unpredictability of the animal's reaction to such things as sounds, sudden movement, and unfamiliar objects, persons, or other animals;

(III) Certain hazards such as surface and subsurface conditions;

(IV) Collisions with other animals or objects;

(V) The potential of a participant to act in a negligent manner that may contribute to injury to the participant or others, such as failing to maintain control over the animal or not acting within his or her ability.

Exceptions in the Laws That May Create Liability

The vast majority of the laws contain specific exceptions which, by their terms, will allow injured parties (or someone on their behalf) to sue under certain limited circumstances. Most *but not all* of the statutes state that an "equine activity sponsor," "equine professional," or possibly others addressed in the statute can be sued if they:

• Provide faulty tack or equipment that somehow causes

86

harm to the equine activity participant.

• Improperly match horse and rider or fail to determine the rider's ability to safely manage the horse based on the representations of his or her abilities.

• Own, lease, or have lawful use of land or facilities that have a dangerous latent (non-obvious) condition but for which no conspicuous warning signs were posted.

• In some states, an exception may allow liability where "gross negligence" or intentional wrongdoing was committed. Other states, including Florida, Maine, Michigan, Utah, and Virginia appear to allow lawsuits to proceed under the basic standard of negligence.

Avoiding Conditions That Could Trigger Liability

The equine liability laws were not designed to permanently end all liability where horse activities are involved. However, the exceptions discussed above specify and limit the circumstances in which a personal injury lawsuit could be brought. As a result, liability can potentially be avoided by understanding *and* actively avoiding the conditions that could trigger the laws' exceptions.

What extra precautions can be taken to avoid liability in a state with a liability law? Taking extra time to inspect tack or equipment; placing noticeable warning signs near areas that are known to have dangerous conditions that riders might not easily spot; obtaining a reasonably detailed explanation of a rider's ability and experience before matching him or her with a horse; understanding the general nature and disposition of each horse used for lessons or rentals; and giving riders basic instruction on steering, stopping, and handling the horse.

Sign and Notice Requirements
Under The Liability Laws

Liability laws in 21 states require certain persons or entities (usually equine activity sponsors or equine professionals) to post certain warning signs containing mandated language. These states are: Alabama, Arkansas, Colorado, Delaware, Florida, Georgia, Illinois, Indiana, Kansas, Louisiana, Massachusetts, Michigan, Minnesota, Mississippi, Missouri, New Mexico, Rhode Island, South Carolina, South Dakota, Texas, and Tennessee.

For example, the warning language mandated in Michigan's law states:

WARNING

Under the Michigan equine activity liability act, an equine professional is not liable for an injury to or the death of a participant in an equine activity resulting from an inherent risk of the equine activity.

Illinois' law requires slightly different language:

WARNING

Under the Equine Activity Liability Act, each participant who engages in an equine activity expressly assumes the risks of engaging in and legal responsibility for injury, loss, or damage to person or property resulting from the risk of equine activities.

Many states also require the warning language to be repeated in contracts and releases, *particularly* when equine professionals use them. To find out whether any of these requirements apply to you, be sure to carefully read a copy of the applicable law.

Compliance with the sign and warning language requirements can be very important. Laws in five states expressly state that those who fail to comply with their sign posting and notice requirements will lose the liability limitations within the laws. Those states are: Alabama, Georgia, Louisiana, Mississippi, and South Carolina.

How are the Laws Faring in Court?

Very few cases have emerged from the courts interpreting or enforcing the existing equine liability laws. Courts in

Tennessee and Washington have already thrown personal injury cases out of court on the strength of those states' equine liability laws. Only Wyoming's law is known to have faced, and lost, a constitutional challenge; however, the Wyoming law differs greatly from those in the other states.

Where Can You Find a Copy of a Law?

Contact your state horse council, state legislator, or lawyer for a copy of a liability law. Also, the citations listed in Part 10 will help you find a copy from a library.

Conclusion

Please keep the following ideas in mind:

1. *Very carefully* read the law that applies in your state and in all states in which you do business. All of the equine liability laws differ, and the differences can be highly significant.

2. The exceptions found within the liability laws override the liability limitations and could allow someone to bring suit against you. Knowing the applicable exceptions will help you take active measures to avoid the liabilities they create.

3. Even if you are not an equine professional or if your liability law does not expressly command you to post warning signs or repeat the warning language in your contracts, it certainly can't hurt to do this anyhow. These actions will help reaffirm to others the existence of the liability law and its liability limitations.

UNDERSTANDING NEGLIGENCE

It has been said: *"All it takes is one personal injury law-suit to force even the most successful horse facility to close its doors for good."* Based on the decreasing number of public riding stables over the past few decades, this statement is truly believable.

Where horses are involved there is virtually unbounded potential for injuries that can happen unpredictably and without a moment's warning. The gentlest horse could spook during a riding lesson and its rider could fall off; a guest could slip and fall down a stairway leading to the hayloft; someone might get kicked by a horse stabled in the barn. When any of these things happen, is somebody negligent?

Defining Negligence

What is negligence? A highly authoritative, widely-accepted definition is found in *Black's Law Dictionary* (5th Edition), which states, in part:

> Negligence is the failure to use such care as a reasonably prudent and careful person would use under similar circumstances; it is the doing of some act which a person of ordinary prudence would not have done under the circumstances or failure to do what a person of ordinary prudence would have done under similar circumstances. Conduct which falls below the standard established by law for the protection of others against unreasonable risk of harm; it is a departure from the conduct expectable of a reasonably prudent person under like circumstances.

90

Put another way, conduct, to be negligent, must fall below a legal standard designed to protect others.

Someone can be negligent, as a matter of law, without even intending to inflict harm on another. This is perhaps the most difficult and frustrating aspect of negligence liability. "Gross negligence" (sometimes compared with "willful and wanton misconduct"), by comparison, is understood in many states to involve an act or omission in reckless disregard of the consequences affecting the life or property of another.

The law recognizes differences between negligence and gross negligence, which can be illustrated by the following examples. A public riding facility that has carelessly forgotten to adjust a horse's cinch before sending him out on the first ride of the day will probably be found negligent if the saddle slips and the rider is injured. The facility that saddles its horses with broken cinches or girth straps, knowing that the equipment could break at any time, will likely be found to have committed acts of gross negligence (or in some states, willful and wanton misconduct) when the equipment breaks and injures the rider.

In evaluating whether negligence exists, courts often consider the foreseeability of harm that may occur when the defendant engaged in the complained-of act or the defendant's failure to act which causes injury to another.

Who Can Be Sued and For How Much?

Inevitably, when a negligence lawsuit is brought, the attorney who represents the one bringing the suit (the "plaintiff") will attempt to sue all possible persons, *particularly* those suspected of being insured or collectible. Potential defendants in a negligence case could include the individual(s) who allegedly caused the injury, the facility where the injury occurred, the owner of the property, and the owner of horse(s) that caused the injury.

The law may also impose liability on parties who did not directly cause the alleged harm. For example, all general partners in a partnership can be liable, and an employer may be liable for its employees who act negligently in performing their job duties.

The money a plaintiff may allowed to receive as compensation for winning a negligence case is called "damages." If a plaintiff can successfully prove that the defendant caused the personal injury and is legally responsible for the resulting harm, the judge or jury w ll then evaluate the amount of damages the plaintiff can recover from the defendant.

In many states, damages in negligence lawsuits can include *but are not limited to* compensation for: the injury suffered; damaged or destroyed personal property; medical and hospital bills; harm to marital relations (called "loss of consortium"); lost past and future earnings; and physical and emotional "pain and suffering." By comparison, if a defendant is found to have acted intentionally or maliciously, courts in several states might order him, her, or a legal entity, to pay the plaintiff "punitive damages." These types of damages are designed to punish the defendant and to discourage similar wrongful conduct by others.

Below are a few examples of some settings in which injured people have, over the years, sued individual horse owners, professionals, and stables for negligence in connection with equine activities:

• *"Vicious or Dangerous" Propensities.* Courts in many states have found people negligent if they knew or had reason to know that a horse had particular dangerous propensities to injure others (through biting, kicking, bolting, or bucking) but failed to take protective action such as post appropriate warning signs, properly restrain or confine the horse, or do other things. Plaintiffs who have brought these types of lawsuits include social guests, prospective horse buyers, lessees and business customers.

Some states have evaluated the challenged conduct of the professional, owner, or keeper as *strict liability* (as opposed to negligence). States that recognize this classification usually require compelling proof that the defendant was sufficiently on notice of the very propensity that injured the plaintiff.

• *Failing to Properly Supervise.* Negligence lawsuits have asserted that the defendant failed to properly supervise the plaintiff, which caused the injury. These types of lawsuits have historically been directed against riding instructors and riding academies.

• *Equipment Defects.* In some cases, negligence may be predicated on the manner in which a horse is equipped to be ridden or used. These cases usually involve defective or improperly-adjusted saddles or harnesses.

• *Unsuitability.* Some negligence cases assert that the defendant (usually a riding stable or professional), failed to properly match the horse and rider, based on the plaintiff/ rider's actual or stated level of ability and experience. Plaintiffs, in these cases, often need to prove that the defendant had a duty to properly match the horse and rider and should have known of the unsuitability.

Defenses

Depending on the facts involved in a particular case and the law that applies in a given state, a defendant can present several possible defenses in response to negligence claims involving personal injuries. These defenses may include *but are not limited to*: the plaintiff's own negligence contributed to the injuries (in Michigan, and approximately 44 other states, this principle is called "comparative negligence," but some states evaluate it differently and term it "contributory negligence"); the defendant's alleged negligence, even if it occurred, did not directly cause the plaintiff's injuries; the danger was "open and obvious" to the plaintiff so no warning was needed; assumption of risk (the plaintiff knew the activity involved was dangerous but proceeded anyway); and/or the plaintiff signed a legally enforceable release of liability.

Conclusion

In conclusion, please keep the following general concepts in mind:

1. *As a general rule, legal liability does not necessarily exist simply because someone was injured on your property.* A negligence case will only succeed if the plaintiff can prove that you failed to act as an "ordinary" or "reasonable" person would have under similar circumstances.

2. Having a basic understanding of what creates liability is an important first step. Beyond this, horse owners and facilities should take active measures to foresee and *prevent*, as much as possible, the conditions that could give rise to injuries and, potentially, liability.

3. To keep better informed of specific ways to avoid liability and to make your operations safer, consider joining groups that are specifically organized to promote safety in equine activities and to share information about safety.

4. Horse facilities, even if they believe they have the "perfect" program to avoid lawsuits and even if their state has adopted an equine liability law, should secure proper insurance. The equine liability laws were not designed to end all lawsuits in the horse industry.

5. Negligence lawsuits are serious, time-consuming, and expensive to defend. If you believe that you may be the target of a negligence lawsuit, or if you seek to further understand how courts in your state have handled negligence lawsuits, consult with a knowledgeable attorney.

PREMISES LIABILITY

What kind of lawsuit could someone bring after he or she was injured on your property? As a classic example, if someone slips and falls in your barn and claims that you were liable, he or she will probably bring a premises liability lawsuit. As discussed below, depending on the state, the person might instead bring suit under an applicable equine liability law.

To evaluate the liability of one who owns land or has legal possession of land (such as a renter) when someone is personally injured on the property requires a focus on the legal classification of the person injured.

Under the law in most states, the plaintiff who brings a premises liability lawsuit must fit within one of three legal categories at the time the injury occurred: *trespasser, licensee/social guest, or invitee.*

Classifying Visitors and Corresponding Duties

• *Trespassers*

Most states' laws provide that those who own or possess land can exercise the lowest standard of care where *trespassers* are involved. There is generally no liability for personal injuries that a trespasser may receive on your property. Liability to a trespasser typically exists if the landowner was grossly negligent or committed an intentional act injuring the trespasser.

The legal duties to a trespasser tend to change, however, if the landowner, in the exercise of ordinary care, knows or should know of a trespasser's presence on the land. In those situations, the landowner or possessor must be very careful before engaging in an activity that could kill or seriously injure a trespasser. This means that the landowner cannot, for example, run a manure spreader directly into trespassers on his land. This also means that if the landowner knows of serious dangers on the property, such as live electrical wires, the landowner may be required by law to take some reasonable action to protect others.

Where child trespassers are involved, a different legal standard usually applies in about two-thirds of the states. These states have followed the doctrine of "attractive nuisance," which is discussed further in this book.

• *Licensees*

With regard to premises liability, many states have adopted the legal classification of licensees. Licensees are people who, directly or indirectly, have received permission to enter the land for their own benefit and not for the landowner's benefit. A social guest whom you invite over for trail riding, for example, probably qualifies as a licensee. The guest of a riding facility's boarder may qualify as a licensee, as well.

Generally, one who owns or is in possession of land owes a licensee a higher duty of care than trespassers. In most states, the landowner's duty to licensees is to use reasonable care to avoid harm and to warn of concealed or hidden dangers of which the landowner actually knows.

* *Invitees*

Invitees, in most states, are owed the highest standard of care by landowners. An invitee is a person who has entered the property with a purpose that can be said to reasonably confer a business, monetary, or tangible benefit on the landowner or possessor. People shopping at stores are invitees; people visiting public horse rental, boarding, and training stables, dude ranches, auctions, and racetracks can also fit within this category.

In most states, a land owner or possessor's legal duty to invitees requires that person to *inspect* the property in order to discover possible dangerous conditions, and then either remove the dangerous conditions or warn invitees of it. Many states have recognized that there is no legally-recognized duty to warn an invitee of a danger that is open and obvious.

The Effect of the Equine Liability Laws on Premises Liability Lawsuits

Has the emergence of equine liability laws caused the end of premises liability lawsuits? The answer is found in the language of the applicable law. To determine whether a particular matter is within the scope of an equine liability law, or whether a matter is instead governed by general principles of negligence or premises liability, it helps to explore the applicable law's terms and definitions.

Most of the equine liability laws state that an equine activity participant cannot bring a suit or recover money from an "equine activity sponsor, equine professional" or other person if the participant is injured as a result of an "inherent risk of an equine activity."

If the injured person was engaged in an "equine activity" at the time of the incident, the equine liability law most likely applies. Also, carefully read the exceptions in the equine liability law. The exceptions allow certain kinds of lawsuits to proceed. One exception commonly found in many states with equine liability statutes allows an "equine activity participant" to sue if an injury has resulted from a "dangerous latent condition of the land." This type of language appears to have replaced the traditional premises liability lawsuit.

Limiting Liability by Other Statutes

Some states have passed laws that limit the liability of landowners and occupiers when someone enters the property to engage in certain types of outdoor recreational activities. For example, Michigan's Recreational Land Use Act [MCL

§ 300.201, *et seq.*] protects owners, tenants, and lessees of large, undeveloped, vacant property kept in a relatively natural state from lawsuits by people who have entered the property for "recreational use" (such as campers, hikers, or snowmobilers).

Under certain specified circumstances, Michigan's recreational land use law eliminates liability for injuries a recreational user might receive on someone else's property *regardless* of whether the user had permission to enter the property. One statutory exception under the Michigan law is if the recreational user paid "valuable consideration" to enter and use of the property. Another exception applies to landowners, tenants, or lessees who, by their own "gross negligence or willful and wanton misconduct," have caused the recreational user to get hurt.

Conclusion

After someone asserts that you are liable, your first step is usually to call a lawyer. However, your efforts to avoid liability can be achieved in partnership with a lawyer. A knowledgeable attorney can explain the law in your state and advise you of the appropriateness and legality of certain measures designed to avoid liability.

Liabilities Involving Children

The law imposes great burdens on landowners to protect children from personal injuries. In many states, the legal duty that a land owner, or one in legal possession of the land, owes to a child who visits the property is to exercise "reasonable or ordinary care" to *prevent* injury. However, the law may require even further action to protect children who enter the property — whether or not they were invited.

Children and "Attractive Nuisances"

Are you liable if a child trespasses on your property and is injured? The answer may depend on what attracted the child to the property.

An "attractive nuisance" is a hazardous place, condition, or thing on the land that, by its features, tends to lure children. Attractive nuisances are typically not natural conditions on the land, such as a pond, but rather are conditions that were *created* by the landowner or someone else on the property. A swimming pool is a classic example. This book further explores the attractive nuisance and how to avoid it.

Children and Liability Releases

Unfortunately, even the best written liability release could fail merely because it involves a child. Under the law in most states, where a child's parent or legal guardian signs a release, the release might only prevent the parent or guardian from bringing the lawsuit. The child might still be permitted to bring a lawsuit on his or her behalf (but laws may govern how old the child must be in order to proceed).

99

The Release Alternative:
Warning Notices

Although a release may not be valid when signed by a child there is no reason why the child cannot be appropriately warned about the risks in equine-related activities. For example, this author has prepared a special form which acknowledges that the child was warned about several equine-related risks.

A risk acknowledgment form is *not* a release of liability — the child's parent or legal guardian (not the child) will sign that document. Rather, the risk acknowledgement form is another part of a risk reduction program that can be implemented by horse owners, professionals, and stables. If the child later sues the stable because of a horse-related incident, the form might reveal that the child agreed to accept the risk that caused the injury or that the child, after receiving the warning, negligently failed to protect himself or herself.

Medical Authorizations

What if a child becomes seriously ill or suffers a major injury while under the stable's supervision? Worse yet, what if the child's parents or legal guardians cannot be found right after this happens? Equine professionals, stables, and summer camps can plan ahead by procuring a proper medical authorization form from the child's parents or legal guardians. These forms allow the person or facility to make important decisions in an emergency. Check the law in your state to determine whether it imposes procedures for medical authorization forms such as witnesses or the seal of a Notary Public.

People and facilities that do not request medical authorization forms would be wise to, at a minimum, get the provider name and policy number for the parents' or guardians' medical insurance.

When Can Children be Liable?

What if a child commits an allegedly negligent act? Can he or she be liable? Possibly.

Resolution of the issue of a child's liability depends on the child's age at the time of the incident. Laws in many states provide, for example, that children under the age of seven (or approximately that age) are legally incapable of being negligent and therefore cannot be sued for negligent conduct. Some states have allowed liability for a child's actions at the age of four.

Determining the liability of a child also depends on the allegedly wrongful act. For example, where the child is alleged to have acted intentionally and wrongfully, many states allow the child to be sued if it can be proven that the child *deliberately* meant to hurt another and fully *understood* that he acted wrongfully at the time he committed the act. Liability under this setting might occur if a child punches someone or inflicts injuries.

When a child engages in certain activities requiring a high degree of responsibility, such as driving a car, his or her conduct is often evaluated by a higher standard of care typically reserved for adults. Consequently, a child driver could be held to the standard of an ordinary and prudent *adult* driver.

AVOIDING THE "ATTRACTIVE NUISANCE"

Trespassing children are any horse facility's nightmare. Children cannot (or simply do not) read warning signs. They are capable of climbing over or crawling under fences. Can the law impose certain responsibilities on horse facilities to protect young children who trespass on their property?

Yes. Most states across the country have adopted the "attractive nuisance" doctrine. Unlike the typical rule that there is generally no duty to protect trespassers, the attractive nuisance doctrine provides that a landowner will be liable for harm caused by artificial conditions of the land that are highly dangerous and, by their features, tend to attract trespassing children.

What is an Attractive Nuisance?

Attractive nuisances are potentially harmful objects and conditions on the land or of the land that, by their features, have the ability to attract children. In most states, attractive nuisances are typically not natural conditions, such as a pond, but rather are conditions that were *created* by the landowner or someone on the property. Examples are swimming pools, sewer drains, tractors, and farm equipment. Depending on the circumstances, horses might also qualify. Young children are unable to understand the dangers these conditions create. Leaving these hazardous conditions in the view and reach of young children will almost certainly tempt the child to approach and meddle with them.

In some states, laws exist that identify certain attractive

nuisance-type hazards and explain how to control them. For example, laws may regulate the storage or disposal of hazardous chemicals (such as pesticides and paints). Also, to protect small children, some laws regulate the height of barbed wire fencing. City ordinances frequently require fencing around swimming pools in order to protect children who wander in the area from drowning. Some ordinances dictate how to discard used refrigerators so that young children cannot play and become trapped inside of them.

When Does Liability Exist?

Some factors courts have considered in evaluating whether a landowner is liable for an attractive nuisance are:

(1) whether the landowner knew or had reason to know that children could trespass near the hazard;

(2) the type of hazard on the property and whether the hazard poses an unreasonable risk of death or serious bodily harm to children;

(3) whether the children, due to their youth, could appreciate the risk involved;

(4) the importance to the landowner of maintaining the hazardous condition;

(5) how the burden of eliminating the hazard compares to the risk of harm involved; and

(6) whether the landowner exercised reasonable care to eliminate the hazard or protect the children.

Very few cases thus far have centered on whether a horse or pony may qualify as an attractive nuisance. However, courts addressing the issue have focused on the animal's basic tendencies. Under this rationale, horses known to be gentle with no known vicious propensities do not create a foreseeable risk of serious injury to others and, therefore, would not qualify as an attractive nuisance.

Defenses

Where an attractive nuisance is involved, landowners will typically base their defenses on the factors listed above. Do not assume that you can successfully defend a case by blaming the childrens' parents for failing to properly supervise them; courts will usually not consider these sufficient to defeat a valid attractive nuisance claim.

Conclusion

Please keep the following concepts in mind:

1. You can take active measures to avoid liability for an attractive nuisance. Check your property regularly to spot the types of hazards that might foreseeably create a risk of injury to others. Evaluate the location of these items and the dangers they may pose. Consider removing the items, moving them away from plain view, placing them in securely locked enclosures, or installing fencing near them.

2. Check your local ordinances, which you can find in your local public library or city hall, for regulations involving fences and storage of items. Make sure you comply.

3. Sometimes, if you fail to take certain precautions required under your insurance policy to protect others from hazards on your property, your insurance coverage might be voided. Ask your insurance agent if your policy requires you to take any special precautions.

4. Your conduct in allowing children to trespass on your property could almost certainly make you liable if an injury results from an attractive nuisance. If you see children trespass across your land, warn them of the possible danger and consider ordering them off of your property. Send their parents a certified letter cautioning them to keep the children away. These efforts, in themselves, will not eliminate your liability, but they will help evidence the many precautions you are taking to protect others.

5. Landowners in some states can be liable for an attractive nuisance without actually knowing that children have trespassed onto their property. Those states, such as Michigan, will make property owners liable if they "had reason to know" that children were likely to trespass and, in the process, get hurt. Consequently, horse facilities located near residential areas or schools may have an extra burden to protect child trespassers from hazards on the land.

6. If you have horses with known dangerous tendencies, securely pasture them away from areas where children could easily see and approach them. When those horses are kept inside, make sure that their stalls are constructed to prevent them from harming or approaching people.

EIGHTEEN SUGGESTIONS FOR AVOIDING LIABILITY

Nobody wants to see anyone injured near horses. By taking active measures *now* to foresee and prevent injuries from occurring, owners of horses and horse facilities *can* prevent injuries from occurring. Also, their guests, employees, and customers can help. The few extra moments taken to detect possible hazards and eliminate them could make all the difference. The following are some suggestions designed to get you started on your way to a safer and more enjoyable facility.

1. Scan barns and pasture areas for exposed nails and sharp corners or objects. Repair them promptly.

2. Commercial horse facilities should try to keep entrance ways as clear as possible of snow and ice.

3. Keep warning signs available and post them where necessary.

4. Place a first aid kit in the barn and advise everyone at the facility where to find it.

5. Post your "stable rules" in the barn and give a copy to each boarder.

6. Keep a note pad or message board available to allow others to leave messages alerting you to problems requiring attention.

7. Install lighting around the stables to keep areas sufficiently lit.

8. Cover or fill in open, gaping holes.

9. Plan regular fence inspections in which all pasture fencing is checked for breaks, loose or exposed nails or unsafe edges.

10. Educate people about ASTM-standard/SEI-certified protective helmets, which are designed for use around horses and in horse-related activities.

11. Keep people who are intoxicated away from horses and horse facilities.

12. Post warning signs near horses known to have vicious or dangerous propensities.

13. Horses having known vicious or dangerous propensities should be pastured away from visitors and placed in secure stalls.

14. Protect or reinforce windows so that horses or people cannot break through them.

15. Use contracts and written releases for horse transactions such as riding lessons, horse rentals, and horse training. Consider updating your existing release forms.

16. Make sure your insurance is up to date as to types and amounts of coverage.

17. Post "no trespassing" signs.

18. Locate electrical and extension cords away from where people might trip on them and out of the reach of horses.

SAFETY HELMETS: IGNORE THEM AT YOUR PERIL

In contact sports like football, where players run, fall, tumble, and collide on level ground, helmets are universally-required gear. However, in horse-related activities — where participants move at tremendous speeds, fall great distances to the ground, travel on rough and sometimes hazardous terrain in distant areas, and handle horses with minds of their own — people often hesitate to wear helmets. People can reduce the risk of serious injury in horse-related activities with the use of safety helmets.

Why Use a Safety Helmet?

Any horse-related activity can deliver a deadly impact to your head if you get kicked or fall. Without protective headgear you may be lucky enough to walk away from an incident with bumps, cuts, and bruises. The fact is, serious damage that you cannot see may already have occurred inside of your head. When you try to resume your normal functions after a head injury, you might discover that you cannot concentrate, your memory is cut short, and you cannot speak or think as well. Sooner or later, you might also find that you cannot see, read, hear, smell, taste, or move as well as you used to. You might have dizzy spells or become more irritable or lethargic. These are often symptoms of "closed head injuries."

Closed head injuries have the potential to be very serious. The more fortunate closed head injury victims will find that their injuries heal over time, but many people will improve only after intensive therapy with drugs or rehabilita-

108

tion. However, others will remain disabled for the rest of their lives.

Safety helmets are designed to cushion and re-distribute the force of certain blows to the head. Wearing a safety helmet could allow you to walk away virtually unharmed from an accident that might otherwise have killed you or required costly long-term care. In other cases, the helmet might greatly reduce the injury.

Are All Safety Helmets Alike?

No. Based on current technology, the helmets proven to best protect you in equine activities comply with Standard 1163 by the American Society for Testing Materials (ASTM) and are certified by the Safety Equipment Institute (SEI). Look for the ASTM and SEI designations on the label, usually attached to the inside shell, before you buy a helmet.

Several manufacturers produce equestrian helmets known to meet ASTM standard of protection and SEI certification. They include: Troxel, Equine Marketing, Ltd., International Riding Helmets, Inc., Lexington Safety Products, Inc. and Soyo International Group.

To work effectively, a helmet must be properly fitted and secured. Helmets should provide a snug yet comfortable fit. Helmets that slide or loosen, even after being strapped on, signal an improper fit. Most equestrian safety helmets are designed to rest in a level position on the head with the front brim about an inch above the eyebrows.

Should You Require Helmets?

The decision is yours. Many organizations already do, such as the United States Pony Club and Girl Scouts. Also, numerous 4-H programs, summer camps, riding instructors, trainers, and stables across the country are requiring participants to wear safety helmets.

At a minimum, it always helps to caution people about the benefits of proper equestrian protective headgear. If you provide safety helmets for others, make sure that they are properly fitted or keep information available with each helmet on how they should fit. Also, consider using washable helmet liners or keeping disinfectants available that are known to prevent the spread of head lice.

Inevitably, people may elect not to wear a helmet. In these instances, if you are providing horses to them or if you are charged with supervising them, consider asking these people to acknowledge *in writing* that you have explained to them the benefits of a proper safety helmet and the risks associated with not wearing one.

Conclusion

In conclusion, please keep the following concepts in mind:

1. Look for the ASTM and SEI initials on the helmet label *before* you buy, which will reflect the equestrian standard of protection and certification. These helmets reduce the risk of head injury compared with helmets of lesser standards.

2. Never borrow someone else's safety helmet unless you are certain that it fits properly. A properly-fitted safety helmet should be snug and never slide and should have a secure harness or strap. Read the manufacturer's instructions or ask your dealer to make sure that you have bought the right size and adjusted the helmet correctly.

3. Do not assume that helmets are only for riding activity. Your helmet might protect you from head injuries that can occur while grooming, leading, or just being near horses.

4. Safety helmets are widely accepted in the show ring. For example, the American Quarter Horse Association recently issued a 1996 rule clarification, which specified that safety helmets and harnesses are acceptable but optional attire in horse shows approved by that organization.

5. Although proper headgear may prevent or lessen the severity of some head injuries, remember that even a safety helmet cannot protect you against all head injuries, especially injuries that occur outside of the helmet area.

6. If people ride your horses or are under your supervision, consider informing them about safety helmets. These people also can be asked to sign an appropriately-worded statement that, at a minimum, acknowledges receiving this information.

HANDLING PERSONAL INJURIES THAT MAY ARISE ON THE PREMISES

Could this situation happen to you?

Your friend wants to ride your horse. She assures you that she is an "experienced rider." Finally, you obliged and allowed her to have a short ride in an arena. Things started out fine at the walk. Within minutes, however, as your friend encouraged your very willing horse to speed up, it became apparent that she had very little riding experience. You calmly asked her to slow to a halt, and you carefully entered the arena to help her dismount. But it was too late. Your friend fell off, breaking her arm.

After the fall your friend exclaimed that "it was all her fault" and that she just lost her balance. She told you that her arm hurt, but she was otherwise feeling "just fine." Nevertheless, you made sure that she proceeded directly to the hospital.

Three years later, your friend has taken you to court. She claims that she now suffers crippling back and neck injuries, that her arm no longer moves properly and she claims that you were negligent for providing a dangerous horse and dangerous equipment. Her lawsuit seeks over $250,000 from you.

The lawsuit in the scenario above was brought nearly three years after the incident and came as a total surprise. In three years' time you may have forgotten your friend's repeated statements that she was an "experienced rider" that "it was all her fault," and that she lost her balance before falling off. You may have forgotten which saddle and bridle

112

you used and that both were completely intact after your friend fell. You may have forgotten that your friend told you and others that she was "just fine" moments after the incident. You may have forgotten who was present when the incident took place or how to reach them.

When you are sued, the passage of time can work to your disadvantage. Careful action taken shortly after the incident, however, can help you retain evidence supporting powerful defenses that could help you win your case.

Handling an Incident

The suggestions listed below are designed to guide you in the unfortunate event that someone experiences an injury on your property or while riding or near one of your horses. Although there is no established formula for how to best handle each situation, keep these points in mind:

Do:

• Act quickly and obtain medical assistance where needed.

• At a minimum, get the injured person's name, address, and phone number. Obtain the same information from each witness.

• If you personally witnessed the incident, try to remember the facts as completely as possible. Consider writing a detailed description.

• Under your insurance policy, you may be obligated to promptly notify your insurer of any incident.

• Direct your questions to your lawyer and your insurance company.

Don't:

• Admit guilt or admit that you were, in any way, negligent.

• Discuss the issue of whether or not you were liable for the incident. Your lawyer and insurer will discuss these issues with you.

• Refuse or withhold medical attention when the injured person needs it. This omission could, on its own, create liability.

• Assume that injured persons will not sue. They can, and (sometimes) they do.

113

Sharing Information

For obvious reasons, any information you may compile or retain regarding an incident will likely become prime evidence in a lawsuit. Keep it in a safe place and do not destroy it unless you are sure that it is not necessary or that the statute of limitations (the time frame established by law in which the suit can be filed) has passed.

If an incident involves a young child, keep in mind that most states allow children to legally bring suit on their own behalf a certain time after they have turned 18. This fact alone should encourage people to keep records safely stored and organized for extended periods.

What if, in the example above, your friend or her lawyer hired an investigator to meet with you before she filed the suit? If this occurs, you would be wise to contact your insurance company or lawyer and obtain permission before attending the meeting and before agreeing to share information.

PART SEVEN

MAXIMIZING THE VALUE OF EQUINE INSURANCE

A GENERAL OVERVIEW OF
EQUINE-RELATED INSURANCE

Understanding equine-related insurance is good horse sense. Making an uninformed decision that you do not need insurance or buying the wrong types and amounts of insurance can be very costly mistakes. There are several different types of equine-related insurance. If you have specific questions about insurance, direct them to your insurance agent.

What Does Insurance Do?

An insurance policy is a contract between the insurance company and you. With some policies, such as mortality insurance, the company agrees to pay you a sum of money if your horse dies or is stolen. With other policies, such as liability insurance, the company can provide legal counsel for you and pay (up to a specific dollar amount) certain demands or judgments against you arising from personal injury or property damage for which someone claims you are legally responsible.

Liability Insurance

Because of the unpredictable nature of horses, and the fact that we live in a society where lawsuits are commonly brought, having proper liability insurance is more important than ever. All it takes is one personal injury lawsuit to drain your savings and end your horse activities for good.

Liability insurance is designed to address certain *unin-*

tentional situations in which someone is injured either on your property, from an act that occurs around your horse (such as a bite, kick, or fall), or in some cases from an injury that arises under your supervision (such as a riding lesson). A liability insurance policy typically provides that the company will handle, up to a specific dollar amount, certain demands, claims, or judgments brought against you.

Several different types of liability insurance are available within the horse industry. Here are a few of them:

• *Homeowner's Insurance.* The standard homeowner's policy usually provides liability insurance, in some amount, which covers unintentional injuries that may occur on your property and unintentional damage to someone else's property. This insurance typically applies if a social visitor slips and falls in your driveway; it might also apply if your horse hurts a social guest or gets loose and injures someone else's property or person.

Homeowner's insurance does *not* cover personal injuries that arise through business activities or "business pursuits" on your premises. If, for example, you train or board horses belonging to others, or if you give riding lessons on your property you will need to buy a separate commercial general equine liability policy.

• *Commercial General Equine Liability.* Every equine business such as a boarding, training, or lesson facility should not be without this type of insurance. Rmember, however, that there are limits to this type of business insurance.

What if you board or train horses belonging to others, and a horse gets loose and is hit by a car? What if a horse founders or colics under your care? Commercial liability policies may not cover these and other situations where someone brings claims against a business for damage to or loss of personal property (a horse). To cover these types of risks, you might want to add "care, custody, and control" insurance to your commercial liability coverage.

Commercial general liability policies almost always exclude injuries to your employees while they are on the job. Worker's compensation insurance covers these incidents.

• *Professional Liability.* What if you train horses or give lessons at someone else's barn? In these instances, you might want to purchase separate liability insurance designed to protect you in the event that someone claims that you were somehow negligent or violated an equine activity liability law in the performance of your duties.

• *Individual Horse Owner's Liability.* Liability insurance is available for the individual horse owner who is not an equine professional and does not stable a horse at home. This type of insurance covers injury or damage that may arise from your horse activities anywhere — trail rides, parades, horse shows, or at the boarding stable.

• *Horse Club Events.* Clubs or associations that organize or sponsor a series of shows or events can purchase a discounted liability policy to cover all of them. Check the coverage, however. These policies usually cover injuries or damage to spectators only and may not apply to claims for injury, death, or damage brought directly by members of the association or an event participant.

• *Single-Day Equine Events.* This insurance applies to a specific equine event such as a show, race, clinic, or exposition.

Equine Mortality Insurance

Equine mortality insurance is like a term life insurance policy on your horse. This type of policy is designed to pay you a sum after your horse has died from illness, injury, disease, or accident. Mortality policies may also provide coverage if your horse is stolen.

Virtually all mortality insurance policies require, as a condition to their issuance, that the horse must be in good health and free from any injury, disease, or disability at the time of the application. Together with the application, insurance companies usually provide a veterinary certificate of exami-

119

nation form. Your veterinarian must examine the horse and complete the form.

People sometimes misunderstand the amount of the mortality insurance they buy. This misunderstanding arises when they fail to read their policies in order to determine whether they have an "actual cash value" or an "agreed value" policy.

To illustrate the difference between an "actual cash value" and "an agreed value" policy, let's follow a claim on a $7,500 policy of mortality insurance issued on the life of a show or race horse. We will assume: the horse owner submitted a proper and timely claim, the loss was covered under the policy, and the insurance company agreed to pay the claim.

If you purchased an "agreed value" mortality insurance policy, there is no question that the insurer would pay you the full $7,500. "Agreed value" policies provide coverage for a specifically agreed-upon amount.

If you purchased an "actual cash value" or fair market value policy, the insurance company might pay you less than $7,500 if it had reason to believe that the lesser amount reflects the fair market value of your horse around the time of its death. While situations like this occur rather infrequently, they illustrate the importance of insuring your horse in an amount that does not exceed its true value.

Equine Health Insurance

Surgical insurance typically covers up to $5,000 in expenses for surgery that a licensed veterinarian may need to perform on your horse. This insurance will not apply if your horse has a pre-existing health condition or if you have submitted your horse to certain types of elective surgery such as castration or a performance-enhancing procedure.

Major medical insurance covers surgery and is also designed to cover (up to a certain amount) diagnostic tests, non-surgical illnesses, and certain other medical care that a licensed veterinarian gives your horse.

Other Types of Insurance

The insurance described below is less common but is nevertheless available from some companies.

• *Breeding Stallion or Mare Infertility.* This policy insures specific breeding stock. For example, the policy may apply when a stallion has become infertile, impotent, or permanently incapable of breeding due to an accident, illness or injury. This type of insurance may also be purchased to provide coverage if a specific mare has become barren.

• *Prospective Foal Insurance.* This policy is purchased on the life of a prospective foal and is designed to cover situations in which the fetus or young foal is aborted, stillborn, or has died from a stated cause.

• *Loss of Use.* Unlike mortality insurance, which pays a sum if your horse dies or is stolen, loss of use insurance applies if your horse is alive but suffers from a physical condition that renders it permanently unable to perform a specific function for which it was insured (such as showing or racing).

• *Specified Perils or Named Perils Insurance.* This policy insures against the loss of a single horse or a herd from specific perils such as transportation accidents, earthquake, lightning, tornado, flood, or others.

Conclusion

In conclusion, please keep the following ideas in mind:

1. *Read your insurance policy very carefully.* All insurance policies differ. Policies cover specific types of harms or "perils" and usually describe them in great detail. Most policies also have specific "exclusions," in which certain perils, persons, activities, or circumstances will not be covered.

2. Make sure that you understand your insurance. For example, if you bought an "umbrella policy," you did not buy extra insurance coverage for extra types of hazards. Rather, you simply increased your policy limits on some or all of your existing insurance to a higher amount. As a result, if your original liability insurance policy had limits of $500,000, your umbrella policy could raise this amount to $1 million and more.

3. Make no assumptions with equine-related insurance. When the insurance agent explains your policy to you, ask him or her to support the explanation with specific policy language. Should a situation arise in which the agent insists that your insurance covers something important, but the agent cannot find policy language to support it, consider asking the agent to confirm the explanation in writing (preferably on his or her professional stationery).

4. Help your insurance agent avoid making assumptions. Show him or her your facility. Explain the types of services you provide, the number and quality of horses you own or keep, and where you transact business. This could directly influence the types and amounts of insurance he or she suggests.

5. When shopping for insurance, the cost of the premium (the price of insurance for a specified risk and a specified length of time) should not be the deciding factor. As mentioned earlier, insurance coverage can differ greatly — even if the policies you are comparing are both mortality insurance. Before you buy, make sure that the cheaper premium reflects coverage identical to the higher premium and that the cheaper insurance is backed by a financially stable company.

FIVE OF THE MOST COMMON EQUINE INSURANCE MISTAKES PEOPLE MAKE AND HOW TO AVOID THEM

Each year, the horse industry, on a national level, spends several million dollars on various types of equine-related insurance policies such as mortality, liability, health (major medical and surgical), and loss of use. Sometimes, the consumer and the insurance company disagree over the issue of whether the company is required to pay or handle certain kinds of claims. People usually learn after it is too late that many of these problems and disputes could have been avoided.

Here are five of the most common mistakes people make, which generate misunderstandings and sometimes legal disputes with their insurance companies:

1. Assuming That Your Homeowner's Insurance Covers Your Equine Business Operations

The basic homeowner's insurance policy is *not* business insurance. A homeowner's insurance policy would likely protect you if a social visitor slipped and fell near your barn. However, the policy might not protect you if the one who fell was a business customer.

Homeowner's policies, by their terms, almost always *exclude* coverage (and therefore will not protect you) if someone is injured in connection with a "business pursuit." Numerous activities in the horse industry could potentially qualify as "business pursuits," such as riding lessons, boarding, or horse training in exchange for money or something of value. These and other types of business activities almost always require separate commercial liability insurance.

123

2. Failing to Timely Notify the Mortality Insurance Company When Your Horse is Injured or Ill

Does your mortality insurance company need to know when your horse is injured, lame, sick, or in an accident? The answer is usually *yes*.

Notifying the insurance company is a very important duty in a mortality insurance policy. This duty is so important that, in some instances, companies will deny payment where they reasonably believe that the policyholder has failed to honor the policy's terms of giving timely and proper notice.

The notice requirements can vary from company to company. Most mortality insurers require policyholders to give "immediate" or "prompt" notice of an insured horse's injury, lameness, or illness. Some policies require notice to the insurer "as soon as practicable."

Even well-intentioned policyholders who are mindful of the notice requirement sometimes assume that the company need not receive notice if, for example, the horse's problem seems under control and the horse is receiving good veterinary attention. This can be a very costly mistake, however, especially if the horse's condition worsens to the point that it must be euthanized (put to sleep). Contacting the insurance company at this advanced stage might be considered too late.

From the standpoint of the insurance company, timely notice serves many important purposes. Upon issuing a mortality insurance policy on your horse, the insurance company has a financial interest in your horse and its well-being. Consequently, the company wants immediate notice of illness, disease, lameness, or injury —usually without regard to the seriousness of the condition.

Many policyholders are surprised to learn that insurance companies actually respond and take action after being notified about a horse's condition. For example, when a horse colics or begins to show signs of wobbling, the insurance company can do any number of things, including: investigate what caused the problem; confer with the attending veterinarian to review the type of medical attention the horse is receiving; order another course of treatment; submit the horse to another veterinarian; determine whether the problem would be covered under the policy in the event that the horse dies or must be destroyed; advise you whether the policy covers the cause of the problem or illness; give consent to euthanize the horse; and/or plan for an immediate post-mortem examination.

3. Failing to Notify the Right Person or Company When an Insured Horse Becomes Injured or Ill

Giving timely notice serves no purpose if the notice is directed to the wrong person or company. Be sure to direct the notice to the exact person or company specified in your insurance policy. The agent who sold you the insurance policy is not always the person to whom your policy requires notification.

4. Failing to Protect the Right People in Your Liability Insurance Policy

Have you ever wondered exactly who your liability insurance policy insures? If you are the only person named on the policy, and consequently the only one the policy is designated to protect in case something happens, proceed to number 5. However, if any of the circumstances below apply to you, it might be necessary to contact your insurance agent about adding other people or entities as "additional named insureds."

• *You operate under a corporate name.* Unless the policy insures that name, there may be no insurance coverage for that entity.

• *Your equine business is a partnership with others.* Since all partners can be individually liable for the business activities of the partnership, the policy should name and insure the partnership and each of its partners.

125

• *Your spouse co-owns the land but may or may not be involved in your equine activities.* Include your spouse's name on the policy just to be safe.

• *Employees or others work for you.* Make sure that your policy will cover the acts of your employees while they are on the job.

• *Someone else owns the land on which you conduct equine activities (such as boarding, training, or instruction).* If you do not own the land but merely use it, you should coordinate with the land owner to determine who has insurance and, if so, exactly who it protects. It may turn out that the land owner is looking to you to buy insurance that will protect him or her, in addition to yourself, if someone is hurt as a result of your use of the land.

5. Assuming That Your Business Liability Insurance Covers an Injury to or Loss of Someone Else's Horse in Your Care, Custody and Control

What happens if a stable is accused of being negligent and causing a boarded horse under its care, custody, and control to colic and die? Will a general commercial liability policy address this situation and protect the stable? Surprisingly, the answer is usually no — unless the stable bought extra insurance commonly known as "care, custody, and control" insurance.

Stables purchase care, custody and control insurance for protection in situations like the one described above in which they are accused of negligently maintaining a horse owned by another but kept in the stable's care custody, and control. The typical general commercial liability policy, without this special type of insurance, would only cover accidents and injuries affecting humans.

Conclusion

In conclusion, please keep the following ideas in mind:

1. Keep important insurance information handy. For example, mortality insurance policies usually give a phone number that you (or someone on your behalf) must call if your horse becomes injured or ill. Keep the number and your policy number in places where you or others who are caring for your horse will have quick access to it. There are numerous possible places, such as near a barn phone (some stables keep an index card file with this information), your wallet, horse trailer, and car.

2. When something is wrong with your horse (or a horse under your care, custody and control), do not hesitate to notify the insurance company because of the lateness of the hour, the day of the week, or a holiday. Mortality insurance companies expect notification calls at any time and, for this reason, designate people to receive them 24 hours a day and 7 days a week.

3. Because of the complexity of insurance disputes, the variety of ways in which they can be handled, and the laws that address them, consult with a lawyer about your matter.

WHY INSURANCE COMPANIES AND LAWYERS SOMETIMES SETTLE CASES OUT OF COURT

A horrible nightmare has come true. A friend fell off your horse during a casual trail ride. Several months later he is suing you. You are positive that you have powerful defenses. The horse at issue, your elderly and practically "bomb-proof" gelding, barely moves and has never thrown a rider. You distinctly recall hearing your friend assure you that he was "100% O.K." after the fall. He even re-mounted and completed the ride. Since the incident, your friend missed no work, has no scars, and his life seems no different than it was before he ever rode your horse.

Let's evaluate two possible responses: *[1] If you have liability insurance, let's assume that your insurance company plans to pay your friend a very small amount of money to settle the case; or [2] If you have no insurance but hired your own lawyer, let's assume that the lawyer recommends that you save the expense of defending the case and instead pay your friend a small sum to settle the case.*

Many people believe that settlements under these and similar circumstances are inappropriate. What reasons would motivate your lawyer or insurance company to suggest a settlement, even if you have valid defenses? Here are some of them:

The High Cost of Defending a Lawsuit

Litigation can be very expensive, and it is extremely difficult to control litigation costs. Plaintiffs' attorneys usually derive their fee from a portion of the money the plaintiff recovers, and they usually waive legal fees if the plaintiff loses; this arrangement is commonly known as a "contingency fee." Defense attorneys do not operate on contingency fees, however, and the obligation of you (or your insurance company) to pay the costs of a legal defense remains the same whether you win or lose the case.

Many people assume that the court will order the loser to pay the winner's legal fees. Unfortunately, this very rarely occurs in the United States legal system, although rules in state and federal courts provide that this should occur if the losing party's case or defense was frivolous. As a practical matter, courts in personal injury cases have been very hesitant to order the plantiff to pay the defendant's legal fees.

The Unpredictability of Jury Verdicts

The jury system has received intense criticism in the 1990's. People have accused juries of not paying attention to the evidence, for injecting their own prejudices into a verdict, for not being representative of the general public (since some people are exempt from jury duty), for forgetting major and pivotal events during a trial, and many other things. Therefore, regardless of whether you are the plaintiff or the defendant, any trial can be a gamble because the outcome is never certain.

Avoiding Possible Bad Precedent

What if you won your case at trial but the other side is appealing the case to a higher court? At this stage, it would seem outlandish to settle the case when it seems you are ahead. However, parties sometimes settle cases simply because of the possibility that an appellate court could issue an adverse decision that would create a bad precedent (guiding authority) for people like you in future cases. The motivation to settle under these circumstances depends, in large part, on the importance of the issues that will likely be decided on appeal, the present state of the law, how the trial proceeded, the chance that the appellate court can be persuaded to rule favorably, and the likely cost of the appeal.

The Complexity of the Lawsuit Compared to the Amount Demanded

What if the plaintiff is demanding a small amount to settle the case, but defeating the case through the court system would require spending several times more than that amount? These circumstances might, in the interests of economics alone, dictate that you save the time, trouble, and money through a settlement.

Conclusion

In conclusion, keep these ideas in mind:

1. *Read your insurance policy carefully.* A small number of insurance policies specify that the company cannot settle a claim or a lawsuit without your approval. Typically, however, policies provide that the insurance company retains the ultimate authority to settle a claim brought against you if the settlement is within the limits of the policy.

2. *Communicate.* If your attorney recommends settlement, ask him or her to explain why. Make sure you understand the explanation you receive.

3. *Seek Advice.* In some instances, it might pay to hire an independent lawyer or specialist to evaluate the case and give an opinion to you and your lawyer. Discuss this option with your lawyer.

4. *Get involved.* Possibly, the notion of settlement might have originated from your own lawyer. Acting with the best of intentions and with a desire to give you the best possible service, the lawyer simply may not understand horses. This could create difficulty in grasping the issues, evaluating the strengths and weaknesses of your case, or locating expert witnesses who could best support your position in the case. This lack of knowledge might prompt the lawyer to believe that your case is weaker than it could actually be.

As someone who understands horses, you can be a valuable source of information to your lawyer. You might be well-situated to help him or her find useful and authoritative articles, books, consultants, and expert witnesses. In particular, if you are paying for your own legal fees, this type of assistance might help your lawyer work more efficiently and, consequently, result in lower legal fees.

PART EIGHT

RESOLVING SIMPLE EQUINE (AND NON-EQUINE) DISPUTES OUT OF COURT

UNDERSTANDING THE MECHANICS AND COSTS OF A TYPICAL LAWSUIT

Sometimes, the costs of litigation (the process of handling a case through the court system) can be financially devastating, even for the one who *wins* the lawsuit. What makes litigation expensive? Answering this question requires an understanding of the general mechanics of a typical personal injury lawsuit. Keep in mind that strategies differ in every lawsuit, which will almost certainly impact costs.

The Process of Litigation

The case begins when the plaintiff (or plantiffs) pays a fee and files a Complaint in the appropriate courthouse, which sets forth why the defendant(s) should be found liable and should be ordered to pay the plaintiff money as compensation. The Complaint and other documents (such as a Summons) are delivered to the defendant, after which the defendant has a limited time to file an Answer along with a list of defenses. Sometimes, the defendant might seek to have the case immediately dismissed if the case was filed in the wrong court, the defendant was not presented (or "served") with the lawsuit papers in a legally-appropriate way, the lawsuit's theories were not legally-recognized, or other reasons.

After the defendant has responded to the lawsuit, a trial can sometimes be the next step. However, in most cases the litigation process is just beginning. At this point the time-consuming process of "discovery" typically begins, in which each party learns the facts and information that the other party will use at trial. Discovery can involve: written questions (called "interrogatories"), which require written answers

135

by the other party within a certain time period; document requests; and depositions, which are a series of questions directed to a party, witness, or expert witness who is sworn to tell the truth.

At any point during the lawsuit, either party might present a "motion," which asks the court to do any number of things, such as: dismiss all or part of the case; grant the plaintiff an immediate judgment; order the other side to provide certain disputed discovery, prevent certain evidence or witnesses from being introduced at trial, or others.

To reduce the court backlog and encourage parties to settle cases, courts often will initiate a settlement conference, which is attended by the parties, their lawyers, and the judge. In addition, many state and federal judges across the country are now ordering their cases to proceed through mandatory pre-trial mediation programs.

In equine-related lawsuits, parties frequently hire expert witnesses to testify at trial and help the jury understand the standard of care that a "reasonable" facility should have followed. Also, in some cases, the plaintiff can be examined, at the defendant's expense and request, by an independent physician or expert who can determine whether the plaintiff's injuries are as serious as he or she claims. Not surprisingly, lawsuits often become a "battle of the experts."

Trials end in a verdict, which will decide whether or not the defendant is liable. If so, the defendant usually will be ordered to pay the plaintiff a sum of money as damages. Both parties in a lawsuit have the opportunity to bring an appeal which seeks to overturn the verdict. Keep in mind, however, that appeals can be very expensive. In many successful appeals the court will order a new trial, forcing some of the litigation process to repeat itself.

Lawsuit Costs — Who Pays?

Can the party who wins a lawsuit recover his or her attorney fees? Possibly, but *very* unlikely. In the relatively few instances where this has been done the court usually followed a specific statute or contract awarding fees to a party, or specifically found the plaintiff's case, or the defendant's defense, to be frivolous. Liability insurance is designed to provide and pay for legal counsel and, up to the policy limits, pay for the amount you might be liable to pay to the one who brought the lawsuit. Without insurance, the party who has been sued is responsible for arranging and paying for a legal defense.

WRITING AN EFFECTIVE DEMAND LETTER

Before you are ready to take a case to court, and *particularly* if you have a minor dispute involving a small amount of money which you plan to handle on your own in a small claims court or through other forms of dispute resolution, consider taking a few minutes to prepare a carefully-written demand letter.

A demand letter is a short, concise letter which explains how you believe you were wronged and why you believe the other side should take the action you request.

If done properly, a demand letter can offer many benefits. For example, the one who receives it might provide the result you want. This could spare you the time, trouble, and cost of proceeding further.

How Do You Write a Demand Letter?

How you write your demand letter is up to you, but here are some suggestions:

1. Write clearly and neatly. Better still, type the letter. Keep your own copy.

2. Be succinct and make your point. A one or two page demand letter usually accomplishes far more than one that rambles on for several pages.

3. Avoid attacking the other person. Clearly, you will be motivated to write a demand letter because you feel someone treated you badly. However, an angrily-written letter will more likely draw an angry response, which benefits nobody. Your goal should be to convince the one who receives the letter to take a serious look at the problem, decide whether he or she has valid defenses, and evaluate how difficult it would be to defend the matter if it proceeded in court or through other means of dispute resolution. The goal of your letter is to create an interest in resolving the matter, not an interest in defeating your case.

4. Stick to the facts. The facts can tell your story if you present them in an understandable way.

5. What are you demanding from the other party? Think this through carefully, and explain it in your letter.

6. To help you decide whether and when to pursue other legal options such as a small claims court case, set a fair deadline in which you expect the other party to respond to you. Include that date in your demand letter. It is unreasonable to state in your letter that the other party's failure to respond to you will be deemed an acceptance of the demand in your letter.

Putting these suggestions to the test, take a look at the examples below. Which demand letter would persuade you?:

- "You are a liar and a cheat. I sold you my mare and let you take her home because you promised to pay me over time. You paid only part. Pay the rest now or else!" **or**

- "Nine months ago we signed a contract which allowed you to buy my four-year-old mare for $3,500, with payments to be made in monthly installments of $350. A copy of our contract is attached. As you are aware, you have paid only $2,100 as of today, and I have not received the last three installments. Over the last few months, you have promised to send the payments, and I have been patient with you. However, I cannot wait any more. Unless I receive the full amount of the four remaining unpaid installments ($1,400) by July 15, 1996, I will have no choice but to file a lawsuit against you or take other action allowed by law."

[NOTE: If your demand letter involves collection of money, particularly if you are writing the demand letter on behalf of someone else, you might be subject to certain debt collection practice laws such as the Federal Fair Debt Collection Practice Act, Title 15 U.S. Code § 1692, *et seq.*, and its counterpart found within the laws of several states.]

7. Consider sending your demand letter by certified mail, return receipt requested. The green post card you will receive after the letter has been sent will tell you when the letter reached its destination and who accepted it. You may also want to send an extra copy of the letter by regular mail.

8. Check the facts carefully before sending out your demand letter. There are risks associated with including incorrect information or wrong assumptions in the letter. Also, sometimes statements or written words could have legal significance (such as admissions of wrongdoing or statements that are against the interest of the person who made them). Lawyers usually can spot these problems or avoid them.

If you believe that your dispute warrants a lawyer's attention, you would be wise to refrain from sending your own demand letter. Your lawyer can handle this for you.

ARBITRATION

"I'll see you in court!" These words usually follow a dispute, and the common assumption is that all legal battles require a lawyer and must be resolved through the traditional court system. Is that assumption true?

No. Arbitration is an increasingly common alternative to the court system.

What is Arbitration?

In an arbitration, the parties agree to have up to three neutral third parties such as a lawyer, retired judge, or company providing alternative dispute resolution services listen to both sides of a case, hear key witnesses, examine important documents, and then render a decision. The parties to the dispute must agree that the arbitrator's decision will be valid and binding. In most types of arbitration, a lawyer can handle your case for you. Other types of arbitration involve the parties themselves and their witnesses, but no attorneys.

What are the Benefits of Arbitration?

Arbitration is usually cheaper and faster than going to court. The process of handling a dispute through the court system (also called "litigation") can be very expensive. In some cases, the cost of litigation can be greater than the amount at stake. Much of these costs arise from the lawyer's time and effort preparing the case for trial. Typically, arbitration proceedings involve less time and preparation.

Arbitration can also be more private than a court proceeding. Because there are no court filings in arbitration, there are no publicly-available records of the arbitration and the amount of the resolution. Arbitration proceedings are held away from a courthouse and are closed to the public.

The arbitration decision can usually be enforced in a court of law if the losing party has failed to comply with its terms. When that occurs, the prevailing party typically files a lawsuit in court to have the arbitration award confirmed. Also, a party who believes the arbitrator exceeded his or her bounds or was biased usually can file a lawsuit to have the arbitration award overturned.

How Can You Get Your Dispute Resolved by Arbitration Rather Than in Court?

Submitting a dispute to arbitration usually takes a mutual agreement of the parties. For example, contracts drafted in the 1990's often require disputes between the parties to be submitted to arbitration by either or both parties. Many agreements make it a point to specify that the arbitrator's decision shall be valid and binding.

After a dispute has arisen, can the parties agree to resolve a dispute through arbitration rather than in court? Yes. However, when parties are embroiled in a legal dispute, it is difficult to get them to agree on *anything*, much less agree to submit the matter to an arbitration. For this reason, it is wise to plan ahead and preserve the right to arbitrate within the parties' contract.

Is Arbitration Always Better than Going to Court?

Not always. Because there is typically less preparation involved in arbitration proceedings, many stones will be left unturned, and there is a greater chance of finding surprises at the arbitration hearing.

Also, arbitrators cannot guarantee or provide certain types of relief. For example, an arbitrator cannot —without the consent of the parties — order that an activity such as a challenged horse sale be stopped. A court, by comparison, might be able to grant this relief through an injunction.

Parties who want to deter similar lawsuits in the future might want their dispute resolved in the court rather than through arbitration. Courts can issue an opinion which could serve as authority (called "precedent") to persuade other courts to decide similar cases or issues the same way. The rulings in most arbitrations do not have this effect. Many people have complained that arbitrators too frequently seek a middle ground or compromise rather than decide the winner or loser, which the court will do.

Not every case is best suited for arbitration. Less complex legal matters frequently work well through the arbitration process.

Where Can You Obtain More Information?

For more information regarding alternatives to the court system such as arbitration, check the phone book for the number of the nearest office of the American Arbitration Association or similar services. Also, many communities have community-based resolution centers or neighborhood justice centers; although these centers rarely offer arbitration services, they might direct you to the proper authority. Check your city hall to find a center near you.

MEDIATION

Mediation is a process in which the parties to a dispute agree to allow one or more unbiased persons to serve as a facilitator to help resolve it. Mediation differs from the traditional court system and the arbitration process; in those settings, a winner or loser emerges. However, the job of a mediator is not to decide who wins or loses. Rather, the mediator encourages both sides to discuss their respective positions and to resolve their disputes.

The mediation process is typically informal. It rarely resembles a trial and often no witnesses must be present. Mediations are usually conducted in an casual and comfortable setting. To encourage openness and mutual cooperation, mediations typically abandon strict rules governing how evidence is presented and the order of presentation. As the mediation proceeds, the parties attempt to work together toward a compromise that is acceptable to all. This compares sharply to the court system in which the parties' relationship often worsens.

Who Benefits from Mediation?

Mediation is especially useful for parties to a dispute who, based on where they live or their line of business, will need to work or do business together in the future. Given these factors, many minor disputes in the horse industry lend themselves well to mediation. Mediation might also be useful to resolve minor disputes in which each party has a competing claim, such as a payment dispute where one party refuses to pay because of claimed misconduct of another.

What Happens After the Mediation?

After a successful mediation, the parties will leave with a freshly-written agreement in hand that completely resolves the dispute. If the mediation was unsuccessful, the parties are free to pursue their matter through the court system (or, sometimes, arbitration).

Is Every Legal Dispute Appropriate for Mediation?

No. Mediation is designed to promote *compromise*. Issues and disputes which are less capable of being resolved by a "middle ground" or compromise are not necessarily appropriate for mediation and are better suited for the court system or arbitration. These types of disputes can include, for example, whether or not the parties had a contract of sale or whether the horse must be sold to one person as opposed to another.

Because mediation is an alternative to the court system, it takes a mutual agreement between the parties to mediate a dispute and to accept a certain location for the mediation. Compared to an arbitration decision, the decision of a mediator may not be enforceable in a court of law.

How Can You Learn More About Mediation?

Chances are good that your community has a community dispute resolution center or a neighborhood justice center. Many of these centers will allow you to schedule a mediation within their offices and will provide a neutral mediator for you, with the consent of all parties. Contact your local courthouse, local library, telephone book, or city hall to locate the center in your area.

SMALL CLAIMS COURT

Most states have a small claims court, although the states may name the court differently. These courts are usually situated within each county and are established to resolve disputes involving rather small amounts of money. Each state differs on the maximum amount of money that is recoverable through (or within the jurisdiction of) a small claims court. The television show known as "The People's Court," which was popular in the 1980's, portrayed the typical process of a small claims court.

What Are the Benefits of Small Claims Court?

Compared to the traditional court system, small claims courts can offer numerous benefits, including:

- *You Act as Your Own Lawyer.* Small claims courts allow people to represent themselves and organize their own legal claims or defenses. In some states, such as California, Michigan, and Nebraska, lawyers are not permitted to represent parties in small claims court.

- *Cost.* Because you will usually handle your own case in a small claims court proceeding, you are spared the burden of paying legal fees.

- *Speed.* In the traditional legal system, you may wait well over one year before your case goes to trial. By comparison, most small claims courts will schedule a hearing, in which the judge will decide your case, within a month or two after the case is filed.

What are the Disadvantages
of Small Claims Court?

Sometimes, the case you file in a small claims court could be more than you bargained for. For example, the one who has been sued (the defendant) has the right to hire a lawyer and/or demand a trial by jury. When either event occurs, many states will automatically transfer the case out of the small claims court division and into the regular division of the court. These circumstances might demand that you hire a lawyer of your own. If this happens, you will begin to pay the legal fees you had intended to avoid.

Also, the party you have sued has the right to bring a claim or claims against you within the same case you filed as long as those claims have arisen out of the same transaction or occurrence of the original lawsuit. This is called a "counterclaim." After a counterclaim is filed against you, you will be required to defend yourself, and the case will have lost its original focus on how the other party wronged you.

What Types of Matters Can Go
to Small Claims Court?

Small claims courts are designed to resolve disputes where relatively small amounts of money are involved. Faulty saddle repairs, unpaid boarding or training fees, or an unpaid installment on the purchase of a horse are examples of disputes that could lend themselves well to small claims court.

The maximum amount recoverable in a small claims court varies from state to state. In Michigan, for example, the maximum dollar amount is currently $1,750. Other states such as California, Georgia, Pennsylvania, and Texas allow people to seek up to $5,000 in a small claims court case. Tennessee allows up to $10,000 and in some instances $15,000.

Where Do You File a Small Claims Case?

Sometimes the small claims court case is filed in the court located near where the defendant resides or does business.

147

Alternatively, in some cases, you might be able to sue in the small claims court district where the incident at issue arose. When in doubt, ask a lawyer or check with the small claims court in which you intend to file your lawsuit. Keep in mind that court clerks and staff cannot provide legal advice but might be able to advise you of any restrictions.

How Do You Handle Your Case?

Your case begins when you pay the court a filing fee, which is usually no more than $45. Courts might even relieve you of the obligation to pay this fee if you can sufficiently prove financial hardship.

The first document you will file is the Complaint (or petition), which lists the basic facts of the dispute and the result the plaintiff is seeking. Small claims courts often provide a standard form on which you can write or type the Complaint. In your Complaint, you will need to specify the basic facts of the dispute, attach copies of certain relevant documents (if any exist), and explain how much money you want the court to order the defendant to pay you.

Once the Complaint is filed, a copy is sent to the defendant (the forwarding procedure is called "service of process") either by certified mail or by hand-delivery, depending on the court rules within the state. Sometimes, the court will handle service of process for you.

The defendant is expected to respond to the Complaint either in person before the judge or in writing. This court appearance is called a hearing or trial. There is typically no jury trial in a small claims court case.

What if the defendant fails to respond to the Complaint or show up for the hearing? In these situations, the court might issue a "default." A default is a document which evidences the defendant's failure to timely respond to the lawsuit. Many courts will, after a default has been filed, allow a hearing to take place in which the court will consider awarding the plaintiff a judgment for the amount he or she seeks. A hearing under these circumstances, among other things, allows the court to examine the circumstances under which the defendant was served process.

Since you will usually serve as your own lawyer in a small claims court proceeding, the burden is on you to investigate your own case and present it yourself at the hearing. If you have witnesses, it usually helps to bring them to the hearing, although many small claims courts might accept sworn statements or affidavits from them.

Be prepared to support your case with important documents. For example, if someone has failed to pay an amount owed under a written contract, produce the contract and a schedule of the payments made. Or, if you have sued because someone has damaged your property, such as a saddle, bring the saddle to your hearing along with estimates for repairing the damage. Consider attaching a copy of the demand letter you sent. Find out if the small claims court has rules which you are expected to follow.

Before the hearing, practice your presentation, and possibly recite it for friends and family members. Consider spending some time watching other people present their cases in small claims court. Stick to the basic facts and explain them as concisely as possible.

What Happens If You Win?

If you win your case, the court will issue a judgment for a certain amount of money. Sometimes, the defendant will pay you the full amount of the judgment on the day of the hearing. This is not, unfortunately, a common occurrence. The law establishes a certain period of time, usually no more than a month, in which the defendant can pursue an appeal of the judgment. Only after that time has passed without an appeal will the judgment become legally enforceable.

A small claims court might direct you to certain state laws governing proper post-judgment collection procedures. Follow these laws carefully. Post-judgment collection laws might govern, for example, how to seize a portion of the defendant's wages from his or her employer (a process known as "garnishment of wages"); how to seize money from the defendant's bank account, and how to arrange to have certain of the defendant's personal property (such as a horse, car, truck, or trailer) or real estate seized and sold off to pay a judgment.

If the defendant lacks a steady job, has no money in the bank, or holds no property exclusively in his or her name, your chances of collecting money to satisfy the judgment are slim to none. However, your judgment still has value. States usually allow the judgment to remain valid for several years, sometimes as many as 10 years. If you are the one who benefits from the judgment, find out how long the judgment will remain valid in the state from which it was issued. Before the judgment expires, be sure to take appropriate measures to re-certify it for an additional period. That way, if the defendant gains money or property later on you can attempt to enforce the judgment.

What Happens If You Lose?

The losing party in a small claims court case usually has the right to appeal the decision to a division of the court that has the power to review, and possibly overturn, the small claims decision. Under the rules in most states, the losing party must file its appeal within a certain amount of time from the date the ruling was issued.

Where Can You Find More Information?

Local libraries have several books designed to help you present or defend a small claims court case. Also, your state or local bar association (these are lawyers groups, most of which provide helpful services and information to the public) might have information or pamphlets on small claims court. Consider consulting with a lawyer before you bring your small claims court case; the lawyer might tell you whether small claims court is appropriate and, if so, he or she might even be able to assist you "behind the scenes."

PART NINE

GLOSSARY OF LEGAL TERMS

GLOSSARY OF LEGAL TERMS

A

Action A legal dispute handled through the court system. Related terms: case or lawsuit.

Affidavit A written statement of a witness in a legal proceeding that is made or signed under an oath.

Agent One who carries on certain lawful activity on behalf of another (the principal), subject to the principal's direction.

Agister's Lien A security interest in another person's horse to secure the payment of a debt that arises from the care and keeping of the horse. Related term: Stablemen's lien.

Appeal A request that a higher court review a decision issued by a lower level court to find errors or irregularities.

Arbitration A process by which a legal dispute is resolved out of court with a neutral person or panel of persons hearing both sides of a case, examining certain evidence, and then rendering a decision that may or may not be binding.

Attractive Nuisance A dangerous condition on or of someone's land that, by its features, has the ability to attract young children onto the property.

B

Bar Association A lawyer organization which is established at the national level (such as the American Bar Association), state level, county and/or city level, or for a special pur-

pose. Bar associations often provide useful information regarding dispute resolution alternatives, lawyer discipline,
lawyer referral services, and various lawyer outreach services that benefit the public.

Breach (of Duty or Contract) A departure, without legal
justification, from conduct that is expected based on a legal
standard or from an obligation that was created by a contract.

C

Case Law The law established by decisions of courts, as
opposed to statutes or other sources.

Civil Case A non-criminal case where a person or entity
sues another.

Claim A legal demand or assertion. When a person asserts
through a legal proceeding that another owes him money or
has some other legal obligation, that person has brought a
claim.

Class Action Lawsuit brought by one or more individuals
on behalf of a larger group of people who are in the same
legal situation.

Code A law established by a legislative body such as a state
house of representatives or senate. Related term: statute.

Complaint The plaintiff's first filing that begins a lawsuit.
The Complaint sets forth the plaintiff's claims against the
defendant. Related term: petition.

Consideration Something of value that is given in exchange
for the other party's promise to fulfill a promise.

Contract A legally-enforceable promise between two or more
parties who have exchanged consideration.

Counsel Lawyers in a case; legal advice.

Counter-claim A claim brought against a plaintiff by a defendant in a lawsuit. In the counterclaim, the defendant sues the plaintiff. Related terms: crossclaim; third-party claim.

Criminal Case A case brought by a government aginst someone who is accused of commiting one or more criminal acts.

Crossclaim A claim made by a defendant in a case against another defendant. Related terms: counterclaim; third-party claim.

D

Damages When a person believes he or she has suffered some sort of loss due to the wrongful actions of another, the monetary compensation allowed by law is known as damages.

Decree Judicial command. Related term: mandate.

Defendant The party against whom a lawsuit is filed. In a criminal case, the defendant is the one accused of committing a crime. Opposite term: plaintiff.

Deposition Out of court testimony taken under oath of a party or witness in a lawsuit, with a court reporter or stenographer simultaneously recording a transcript of the testimony.

Discovery The exchange of information in a lawsuit between the parties.

E-F

Federal Case A case filed in a Federal Court, which, by law, must involve either: (1) a legal dispute between residents of two or more different states and the amount of $50,000 or more in controversy; or (2) an alleged violation of a U.S. Constitutional right (such as a First Amendment freedom of speech) or a federal statute (such as the Americans With Disabilities Act, federal securities laws, etc.).

Finding A conclusion reached by a judge or a jury.

Fraud The deceptive words or conduct of a person, upon which another person has relied to his or her detriment, which is designed to deprive the other person of money or something of value.

G-H

Garnishment Proceedings through which a creditor who has a judgment against a defendant can seize certain of the defendant's wages or property in order to pay the debt created by the judgment.

Hearsay Second-hand evidence in which a witness has repeated statements made by others.

Holding A judge's legal conclusion.

I-J

Indemnification An arrangement in which someone agrees to compensate another for an anticipated loss or liability. Some indemnification agreements provide that Person A agrees to pay the legal fees or expenses of Person B in the event that a lawsuit is ever brought against Person B due to the wrongful acts of Person A.

Injunction An order issued by a court that either prevents or compels someone to take a specific type of action.

Issue A point of dispute between two parties in a legal matter.

Jurisdiction A court's power to hear and decide a legal dispute.

Jury A number of people (the amount of which is set by law) who are sworn to examine certain matters and evidence and declare what is true. Juries can decide the outcome of civil or criminal cases.

L

Lawsuit A legal action brought by a plaintiff against a defendant in a court of law.

Lessee One who has received the property of another for a certain period of time. Opposite term: lessor.

Lessor One who leases out property to another for a certain period of time. Opposite term: lessee.

Liable Having legal responsibility.

Libel A written publication such as a book, writing, sign, photograph, or other type of writing that injures a person's character or reputation. Related term: slander.

Litigant An individual or business entity involved in a legal dispute. Related terms: plaintiff, defendant, or party.

Litigation A lawsuit, or the process of handling a lawsuit.

M

Mandate Judicial command. Related term: decree.

Mediation A process in which two disputing parties agree to allow a neutral person or panel of persons to evaluate the dispute and to persuade the parties to settle their differences.

Minor Someone under the legal age in which the law deems them competent to make certain decisions or sign legal documents. Most states have established that minors are under the age of 18.

Motion Request that the judge take a certain action.

N

Negligence An allegation that another person fell below an established standard designed to protect another from an unreasonable risk of harm. The doing of some act which a person of ordinary prudence would not have done under similar circumstances.

Notary Public A public officer capable of administering oaths and performing other official acts. In many states, a Notary Public must observe witnesses or parties sign official or important documents.

Nuisance The use of property or a condition of land that substantially interferes with the use and enjoyment of another's property.

Nuisance Lawsuit A lawsuit brought by one or more nearby landowners seeking to end or abate the nuisance in some way. The words "nuisance lawsuit" have also been applied over the years to describe any type of lawsuit that is brought without justification and serves as an annoyance or nuisance to the one against whom the suit is brought.

O-P

Opinion A decision issued by a court.

Ordinance A law passed by a municipal entity, which typically involves zoning and land use, building, and matters of public safety.

Party or Parties The individuals or business entities involved in a legal dispute. Related terms: plaintiff, defendant, or litigant.

Petition The plaintiff's first filing that begins a lawsuit. Related term: Complaint.

Plaintiff One who brings a lawsuit against another.

Precedent Previous legal decisions that guide subsequent cases.

Presumption A rule of law allowing the court to derive inferences from evidence of a certain type until the truth of an inference has been disproved. For example, many courts will presume that a properly-addressed letter placed in a mail receptacle will arrive at its destination within a certain period of time; the recipient must prove otherwise.

Principal Where an agency relationship is involved, a principal is one who has permitted or directed another person (known as the "agent") to act for his benefit and under his supervision and control.

Private Nuisance A lawsuit alleging nuisance liability brought by a nearby landowner. Related term: public nuisance.

Promissory Note A written document in which a borrower acknowledges a debt and promises payment to the lender under certain terms.

Pro se Representing yourself in a lawsuit. Related terms: *In pro per.*

Proximate Cause The legally-sufficient connection between a person's negligence and another person's injury.

Public Nuisance A lawsuit alleging nuisance liability brought by a group of nearby landowners. Related term: private nuisance.

Q R S

Release of Liability A document in which a person of legal age agrees to give up a right or claim against another. Many states allow a party to release away, and thus relinquish, the right to sue for certain acts or ordinary negligence of another. Related term: waiver.

Ruling A judge's decision.

Settlement An agreement by which the parties dispose of a lawsuit or a dispute.

Slander Spoken words that injure a person's character or reputation. Related term: libel.

Small Claims Court A court which provides an expeditious and informal way of resolving minor claims. The parties usually represent themselves, but many states allow lawyers to be present.

Stablemen's Lien See agister's lien.

Statute A law established by a legislative body such as congress or a state house or senate body. Related term: code.

Statute of Limitations The time period allowed by law for a party to bring certain types of claims in a court of law or legal proceeding against a defendant. After this time period has passed, no lawsuit can be filed.

Summons A formal, written notice advising a defendant that he or she has been sued and/or must appear in court or respond to the lawsuit within a stated time period.

Supreme Court In most states, this is the highest court to which an appeal can be taken. This is the highest court in the federal government.

T U V

Third-party Claim A claim made by a defendant in a case against a party who was not originally named as a party in the lawsuit; the defendant commences a third-party claim when he or she brings claims against that party and brings that party into the lawsuit. Related terms: counterclaim; crossclaim.

Tort A wrong that was committed upon the person or property of another, for which the law recognizes a right to bring suit. A tort is not a violation of a contract.

Trespasser One who enters the property of another without permission or legal justification.

Usury Charging an unlawfully high interest rate.

Venue The county or location in which a court with jurisdiction can hear and decide a legal dispute.

Verdict The jury's decision.

W X Y & Z

Waiver The relinquishment of a right or claim against another. Many states allow a party to waive the right to sue for certain acts or ordinary negligence of another. The waiver can be done in writing or by a course of conduct. Related terms: release of liability.

Warranty A statement that is made in writing or verbally upon which another relies that forms the basis of a sale; usually, the statement is that the product or thing being sold has certain qualities, such as: "The horse does not crib" or "The horse has never taken a lame step in his life."

Witness One who gives testimony under oath about something he or she knew, saw, or heard that is relevant to a lawsuit.

Zoning Regulations issued by municipal entities such as cities, villages, or townships that indicate how real property can be used in different areas and for different purposes.

PART TEN

LIABILITY LAWS INVOLVING EQUINE ACTIVITIES

Equine
&
Law

HORSE
SENSE

Liability Laws Involving Equine Activities

(As of November 1995)

Alabama   Ala. Code §6-5-337 (1993)

Arizona   1994 Ariz. Legisl. Serv. 259

Arkansas   Ark. Code Ch. 120 § 16-120-201,
                   et seq.(1995)

Colorado   Colo. Rev. Stat. § 13-21-119 (1990)

Connecticut   1993 Conn. Acts Pub. Act 93-286

Delaware   Del. Code Anno. Title 10, §8140 (1995)

Florida   1993 Fla. Laws Ch. 93-169, § 773.01,
                   et seq.

Georgia   Ga. Code Anno. § 62-2701 (1991)

Hawaii   1994 Hawaii Sess. Laws 249

Idaho   Id. Code Ch. 18, § 6-1801, *et seq.* (1990)

Illinois   Ill. Stat. Ch. 745 § 47/1 (1995)

Indiana   1995 Ind. Acts 1551

Kansas   1994 Ks. Sess. Laws 290 (1994)

Louisiana   La. Rev. Stat. § 9:2795.1 (1992)

Maine   Me. Rev. Stat. tit. 7 §4101, *et seq.* (1992)

Massachusetts Mass. Gen. Laws Anno. Ch. 128 § 2D
                   (West 1992)

Michigan	Mich. Comp. Laws, §691.1661, *et seq.* (1995)
Minnesota	Minn. Stat. Ch. 623, Art. 3 § 2 (78th Legislature, 1994)
Mississippi	1994 Miss. Laws 443
Missouri	Mo. Revised Statutes § 537.325 (1994)
Montana	Mont. Code Anno. § 27-1-725 (1994)
New Mexico	N. M. Stat. Anno. Art. 13 § 42-13-1, *et seq.* (1993)
North Dakota	N. Dakota Cent. Code § 53-10-1 (1991)
Oregon	Or. Rev. Stat. § 30.687, *et seq.* (1991)
Rhode Island	R. I. Gen. Laws, Ch. 21, § 4-21-1 (1993)
South Carolina	S.C. Code Anno. § 47-9-710 (Lawyers Co-op. 1993)
South Dakota	S. D. Cod. Laws Anno. § 42-11-1 (1993)
Tennessee	Tenn. Code Anno. § 44-20-101 (1992)
Texas	1995 Texas H.B. 280
Utah	Utah Code Anno. § 78-27b-101 (1992)
Virginia	Va. Code Ch. 27.5, § 3.1-796.130 (1991)
Washington	Wash. Rev. Code Anno. § 4.24.530 (1989)
West Virginia	W. Va. Code, art. 4 § 20-4-1 (1990)
Wisconsin	Wisc. Stat. Anno. §895.525 (1988)
Wyoming	Wyo. Stat. § 1-1-122 (1993)

JULIE I. FERSHTMAN MAY BE AVAILABLE TO SPEAK
AT YOUR NEXT CONVENTION

Julie I. Fershtman, the author of *Equine Law & Horse Sense*, is an accomplished speaker on a variety of equine legal topics including: Risk Reduction Strategies, Contracts, Releases, Liability in Equine Activities, Understanding the National Equine Liability Laws, Liability and the Riding Instructor, Liability in Carriage Activities, Legal Transactions in the Horse Business, Avoiding Equine Insurance Mistakes, Avoiding the Attractive Nuisance — *and many others!*

Please send me information regarding the current rates for speeches by Julie I. Fershtman, Attorney at Law

Name:_____

Organization/Company Name:_____

Address: _____

City: _____ State: _____ Zip: _____

Telephone: (___)_____

Fax: (___)_____

Date of Speech Proposed: _____

Organizer/Sponsor of Event: _____

Location of Event: _____

MAIL TO: Horses & The Law Publishing
          P.O. Box 250696
          Franklin, MI 48025-0696
or
FAX TO: (810) 644-8344

IMPORTANT NOTE: This is not presented as a solicitation for the performance of legal services in any jurisdiction. Please remember that speeches are provided for informational and educational purposes only; a speech does not constitute legal advice for any given person or situation.

JULIE I. FERSHTMAN MAY BE AVAILABLE TO SPEAK AT YOUR NEXT CONVENTION

Julie I. Fershtman, the author of *Equine Law & Horse Sense*, is an accomplished speaker on a variety of equine legal topics including: Risk Reduction Strategies, Contracts, Releases, Liability in Equine Activities, Understanding the National Equine Liability Laws, Liability and the Riding Instructor, Liability in Carriage Activities, Legal Transactions in the Horse Business, Avoiding Equine Insurance Mistakes, Avoiding the Attractive Nuisance — *and many others!*

Please send me information regarding the current rates for speeches by Julie I. Fershtman, Attorney at Law

Name:_____

Organization/Company Name:_____

Address: _____

City: _____ State: _____ Zip: _____

Telephone: (____)_____

Fax: (____)_____

Date of Speech Proposed: _____

Organizer/Sponsor of Event: _____

Location of Event: _____

MAIL TO: Horses & The Law Publishing
           P.O. Box 250696
           Franklin, MI 48025-0696
or
FAX TO: (810) 644-8344

IMPORTANT NOTE: This is not presented as a solicitation for the performance of legal services in any jurisdiction. Please remember that speeches are provided for informational and educational purposes only; a speech does not constitute legal advice for any given person or situation.

READER COMMENT FORM
Equine Law & Horse Sense

We've tried to make this publication as useful, accurate, and readable as possible. Please take 5 minutes to tell us if we succeeded. Your comments and suggestions will help us improve our publications. Thank you!

1. HOW DID YOU RECEIVE THIS PUBLICATION?

Meeting/convention (Specify Name and Date)

_____

_____

__ Book store
__ Gift
__ Phone order
__ Mail order
__ Other:
    Describe _____

_____

_____

2. PLEASE RATE THIS PUBLICATION AS FOLLOWS:

__ Excellent __ Good __ Fair __ Poor

Readability
    Was the book easy to understand? __ Yes __ No

Content
    Did the book meet your expectations? __ Yes __ No

    What topics would you like to see covered in Ms. Fershtman's next book?

_____

_____

_____

_____

Appearance
What did you think of the book's appearance?
_____
_____

Would you recommend this book to your friends?
__ Yes __ No

Do you have other comments or suggestions?
_____
_____
_____
_____
_____
_____

Name: _____
Address: _____
City/State/Zip: _____
Phone: _____

Favorite Equine Activities: _____
Favorite Equine Magazines: _____
Favorite Breed(s) of Horses: _____

We appreciate your time and help!

Please return to: Horses & The Law Publishing
P.O. Box 250696
Franklin, MI 48025-0696